The Brazilian Industrial Economy

The Brazilian Industrial Economy

William G. Tyler
Brazilian Planning Secretariat
and University of Florida

LexingtonBooks
D.C. Heath and Company
Lexington, Massachusetts
Toronto

Library of Congress Cataloging in Publication Data

Tyler, William G
The Brazilian industrial economy.

Bibliography: p.
Includes index.
I. Brazil—Industries. 2. Industry and state—Brazil. 3. Industrial promotion—Brazil. I. Title.
HC187.T89 338.0981 79-5440
ISBN 0-669-03448-7 AACR2

Published simultaneously in Canada

Printed in the United States of America

International Standard Book Number: 0-669-03448-7

Library of Congress Catalog Card Number: 79-5440

For David and Elena

Contents

List of Figures and Tables

Figures

Tables

List of Abbreviations and Acronyms

ABDIB	Brazilian Association for the Development of Basic Industry (Associação Brasileira para o Desenvolvimento da Indústria de Base).
ABIMAQ	Brazilian Association of Machine Tool Industries (Associação Brasileira das Indústrias de Máquinas e Ferramentas).
ABINEE	Brazilian Association of Electrical Equipment Industries (Associação Brasileira das Indústrias de Equipamentos Elétricos).
APA	Projects with Agents Program of BNDE (Área de Projetos com Agentes).
BEFIEX	Commission for Granting Fiscal Benefits to Special Export Programs (Comissão para Concessão de Benefícios Fiscais a Programas Especiais de Exportação).
BNB	Bank of the Northeast (Banco do Nordeste do Brasil).
BNDE	National Development Bank (Banco Nacional de Desenvolvimento Econômico).
CACEX	Foreign Trade Department of the Bank of Brazil (Carteira para Comércio Exterior).
CEAG	Center for Managerial Assistance (Centro de Apoio Gerencial).
CEBRAE	Brazilian Center for Assistance to Small and Medium Enterprise (Centro Brasileiro de Apoio à Pequena e Média Empresa).
CDE	Council for Economic Development (Conselho de Desenvolvimento Econômico).
CDI	Council for Industrial Development (Conselho de Desenvolvimento Industrial).
CIEF	Center for Economic and Fiscal Information of the Ministry of Finance (Centro de Informações Econômico-Fiscais).
CIP	Interministerial Price Council (Conselho Interministerial de Preços).
CONSIDER	Council for Steel and Nonferrous Metals (Conselho de Não-Ferrosos e de Siderurgia).
CPA	Council for Tariff Policy (Conselho de Política Aduaneira).
EMBRAER	Brazilian Aeronautical Corporation (Empresa Brasileira de Aeronáutica S.A).

EMBRAMEC	Brazilian Mechanical Corporation (Empresa Brasileira de Mecânica S.A).
EMBRATUR	Brazilian Tourism Corporation (Empresa Brasileira de Turismo S.A).
FINAME	Special Agency for Industrial Financing of BNDE (Agência Especial de Financiamento Industrial).
FINEP	Studies and Projects Financing Agency (Financiadora de Estudos e Projetos).
FINEX	Export Financing Fund of CACEX (Financiadora de Exportações).
FIPE	Economic Research Institute of the University of São Paulo (Fundação Instituto de Pesquisas Econômicas).
FIPEME	Fund for Financing Small and Medium-Sized Enterprise (Fundo de Financiamento à Pequena e Média Empresa).
GERES	Executive Group for the Economic Recovery of the State of Espírito Santo (Grupo Executivo de Recuperação Econômica do Estado do Espírito Santo).
IBDF	Brazilian Institute of Forestry Development (Instituto Brasileiro de Desenvolvimento Florestal).
IBGE	Brazilian Geographic and Statistical Institute (Instituto Brasileiro de Geografia e Estatística).
ICM	Value-Added Sales Tax (Imposto de Circulação de Mercadorias).
IPEA	Institute for Economic and Social Planning of the Planning Secretariat (Instituto de Planejamento Econômico e Social).
IPI	Industrial Product Tax (Imposto de Produtos Industrializados).
MOBRAL	Brazilian Literacy Campaign (Movimento Brasileiro de Alfabetização).
MVR	Standard Reference Value (Maior Valor de Referência).
NBM	Brazilian Product Classification (Nomenclatura Brasileira de Mercadorias).
ORTN	Readjustable National Treasury Bonds (Obrigações Reajustáveis do Tesouro Nacional).
PCIS	Program for Supplementary Industrial Credit of BNB (Programa de Crédito Industrial Suplementas).
POC	Joint Operations Program of BNDE (Programa de Operações Conjuntas).
PROGIRO	Program for Working Capital (Programa de Capital de Giro).
SEPLAN	Planning Secretariat (Secretaria de Planejamento).
SME	Small and Medium-Sized Enterprise.

SMI	Small and Medium-Sized Industry.
SSE	Small Scale Enterprise.
SUDAM	Superintendency for the Development of the Amazon (Superintendência do Desenvolvimento da Amazônia).
SUDENE	Superintendency for the Development of the Northeast (Superintendência do Desenvolvimento do Nordeste).
SUDEPE	Superintendency for the Development of Fishing (Superintendência do Desenvolvimento de Pesca).
SUFRAMA	Superintendency for the Free Port of Manaus (Superintendência para a Zona Franca de Manaus).

Preface

In the past several years I have been engaged in a number of research efforts dealing with the Brazilian industrial sector. This book represents an attempt to bring together under one cover some of the various strains of this research. Accordingly, the chapters can be considered self-contained. If there is a central, underlying theme discernible in the separate chapters, it could be expressed as: the observed vitality of the Brazilian industrial economy has been conditioned by market forces, as sometimes modified and distorted, however, by government policies.

Chapter 1 is an outgrowth and extension of my article "Brazilian Industrialization and Industrial Policies: A Survey" in *World Development*, 4, no. 10/11 (November 1976), and presents an overview of current industrialization problems and industrial policies. There have been sweeping changes in the overall orientation of Brazilian industrial policies since the mid-1970s and any attempt to examine the current situation in the Brazilian industrial sector must take these important changes into account. Chapter 2 deals with the effects of various economic policies on relative prices for the capital-goods sector. Originally researched as part of a project for the World Bank, an earlier version of this chapter was published in Portuguese as "Restrições à Importação e Incentivos Fiscais para o Setor de Bens de Capital no Brasil: 1975/79" in *Pesquisa e Planejamento Econômico*. Chapter 3, dealing with small-scale industry, was also written with World Bank support, and an earlier version appeared in *Financing Development in Latin America*, edited by Jean-Claude Garcia-Zamor and Stewart E. Sutin.

In addition to expressing my gratitude to these publishers for permission to reprint my work, I would like to thank the large number of individuals who assisted me in one way or another during the various stages of the collection of materials, the conduct of the research, and the presentation of the results. Deserving special mention are Irwin Baskind, Xavier Simon, and Wilson Suzigan. My secretary, Odete Fares, has cheerfully endured my sour disposition and provided invaluable assistance in the preparation of the final manuscript. Finally, a debt of gratitude goes to the Research Institute of the Brazilian Planning Secretariat, which has provided generous hospitality, excellent facilities, stimulating colleagues, and a superior research environment. The responsibility for the contents of the volume is entirely my own, and the expressed opinions cannot be interpreted as those of any institution with which I have been affiliated.

1 An Overview of Recent Brazilian Industrialization and Industrial Policies

Introduction: Macroeconomic Considerations

Overall Economic Growth

In discussions of economic development, it has been fashionable among social scientists, journalists, policymakers, and international civil servants to make a distinction between developed and less-developed countries. The dividing line between the two categories has long been recognized as arbitrary and highly subjective. Yet, as long as the so-called less-developed countries had more in common with each other than with the developed countries, the division was largely unquestioned. In recent years, however, the rapid growth of a number of the less-developed countries has rendered the dichotomy far less useful. Countries such as Singapore, Spain, Taiwan, Hong Kong, Korea, and Brazil have achieved high and sustained rates of industrial and economic growth, transforming their economies and reducing the per capita income gap between themselves and the developed countries. These and other countries, sometimes referred to collectively as the semi-industrialized or newly industrialized countries, possess economic characteristics of both developed and less-developed nations. With the possible exceptions of the city-states of Hong Kong and Singapore, the overlapping between the two basic categories reflects the dual nature of the economies of the semi-industrialized countries. Sophisticated and extensive industrial sectors constituting modern enclaves have been developed, while the traditional, and usually agrarian-based, segments of both the economy and society as a whole have been left largely intact.

Brazil is easily characterized as such a dual-economy country. It possesses a large and highly diversified industrial sector, producing a wide range of consumer and producer goods. In fact, on an absolute basis, the total value of Brazil's industrial output is exceeded only by that of a small handful of eight developed countries. By 1978 the industrial sector accounted for a full 37 percent of Brazil's GDP, as compared to 34 percent for the United States.[1] The fact is that Brazil has become industrialized, while at the same time still retaining many of the vestiges of a very poor economy.

Portions of chapter 1 have been incorporated from the author's earlier paper, "Brazilian Industrialization and Industrial Policies: A Survey," *World Development* 4, no. 10/11 (November 1976). Reprinted with permission.

Brazil had increased its per capita income to a level of U.S. $1,570 by 1978, ranking itself higher than a number of the so-called successful developing countries such as Korea ($1,160), Mexico ($1,290), and Taiwan ($1,400), but still less than any of the developed countries [for example, Ireland ($3,470) and Italy ($3,860)].[2] The aggregate, that is, average, income levels disguise the dual character of the Brazilian economy. The rapid and impressive industrialization and economic progress has been concentrated both geographically and socially. Large geographic areas and segments of the population, consisting mostly of the rural poor, have simply been bypassed by the growth of the modern sector. For example, it has been estimated that in 1977 only 20 percent of the Northeast's population aged fifteen years and above could be considered "functionally" literate; that is, as having completed five or more years of schooling. For Brazil as a whole and for the *rural* Northeast the comparable figures were 34 percent and 4 percent, respectively.[3] Similarly, a full 30 percent of the children in the Northeast were estimated to be suffering from second- or third-degree malnutrition.[4]

The overall growth and modernization is not purely a recent phenomenon. The roots of Brazilian industrialization go back to the late nineteenth century, and it has been estimated that by 1919 64 percent of total manufacturing product consumption was produced domestically.[5] While industrial output growth was relatively modest during the 1920s, Brazil experienced a great spurt in its industrial and aggregate economy in the early 1930s. Since that period, with some fluctuations, the economy has enjoyed constant and relatively rapid expansion. Between 1932 and 1979 the average annual rate of growth for GNP and industrial output were 6.3 and 9.0 percent, respectively.

Brazilian economic and industrial history over the past 50 years contains numerous similarities to that of many late-developing European countries of the late nineteenth and early twentieth centuries. One recent analysis (Tyler 1976) has argued that the Brazilian experience is consistent with the Gerschenkronian theory of late development. A central tenet of the latecomer thesis is that countries which have had their industrialization delayed can be benefited in their growth through the use of the technology developed by the pioneers.[6] Brazil has indeed witnessed a sudden great spurt of growth, followed by very high rates of manufacturing growth. There has been a heavy emphasis on large plants in the industrialization drive, and producer goods output, involving heavy industry, has been stressed. Consumption levels have been squeezed by chronic inflation in combination with the existence of a surplus labor economy. Moreover, given the nature of the agricultural labor surplus and the economic policies pursued by the government, the role of agriculture in Brazil's growth over the last 50 years has been accommodative rather than stimulatory. Accordingly, agricultural labor productivity has increased very slowly. Also consistent with the Gerschenkron latecomer thesis has been the pragmatic bending of institutional factors, clearly witnessed in Brazil in the establishment of new forms of public administration to push industrialization, the formation of public enterprises, and the attraction of foreign manufacturing firms.

Following World War II, industrial promotion was emphasized by policymakers, and numerous institutional and policy arrangements were adopted which had the effect of drawing economic resources into industrial activities. Industry emerged as clearly the key sector in the economy, with an established base and with industrial growth rates substantially higher than those of other sectors (table 1-1). The policies promoting this industrial expansion, as discussed in the following section, were highly protectionistic. While these policies for a while contributed to substantial economic growth, economic difficulties, reflecting policy distortions, became increasingly evident.

Table 1-1
Macro-Performance of the Brazilian Economy, 1948-1980

	Annual Growth Rates (percent)						
Year	*GDP*	*GDP per capita*	*Industry*	*Agriculture*	*Exports (U.S. million)*	*Imports (U.S. million)*	*Annual rate of inflation*[a] *(percent)*
1948-1950	6.8	4.3	11.0	4.3	1,210	1,987	12.0
1951-1955	6.8	3.7	7.7	5.1	1,488	645	15.6
1956-1960	6.9	3.7	10.1	3.8	1,333	1,382	20.6
1961	10.3	7.2	10.6	7.6	1,403	1,460	33.3
1962	5.3	2.3	7.8	5.5	1,214	1,475	54.8
1963	1.5	−1.3	0.2	1.0	1,406	1,486	78.0
1964	2.9	0.0	5.2	1.3	1,429	1,263	87.0
1965	2.7	−0.1	−4.7	13.8	1,595	1,096	55.4
1966	3.8	0.8	9.9	−14.6	1,741	1,494	39.5
1967	4.8	1.9	3.1	9.2	1,654	1,667	28.8
1968	11.2	8.1	13.3	4.5	1,881	2,132	27.8
1969	10.0	6.8	12.2	3.8	2,311	2,265	20.3
1970	8.8	5.8	10.0	1.0	2,739	2,849	18.2
1971	13.3	10.2	14.3	11.4	2,904	3,701	17.3
1972	11.7	8.7	13.4	4.2	2,991	4,232	17.4
1973	14.0	10.8	15.8	3.5	6,198	6,192	20.4
1974	9.8	6.8	9.8	8.5	8,568	12,641	31.5
1975	5.6	2.8	6.2	3.4	8,669	12,210	32.7
1976	9.0	6.0	10.8	4.2	10,128	12,383	41.9
1977	4.7	1.8	3.9	9.6	12,120	12.023	42.2
1978	6.0	3.1	8.1	−1.7	12,658	13,683	41.9
1979[b]	6.4	3.5	6.9	3.2	15,244	18,083	55.6
1980[b]	8.0	5.4	8.0	6.8	20,132	22,961	100.2

Sources: Centro de Contas Nacionais of the Fundação Getúlio Vargas, *Atualização Parcial do Sistema de Contas Nacionais,* 1971/72, June 1973; IBGE, *Anuário Estatístico,* 1972; and Fundação Getúlio Vargas, *Conjunctura Econômica,* various issues.

[a]Implicit deflator used in the national income accounts.

[b]Preliminary estimates.

Both agriculture and exports were heavily discriminated against by the constellation of economic policies pursued during the 1950s and early 1960s. Despite rapidly growing world trade, Brazilian exports during this period were virtually stagnant, both with respect to value and commodity composition. From the end of World War II until the early 1960s Brazilian exports, dominated by coffee, averaged a fairly stable $1.3 billion. The growth of the economy, the changing import composition, and increased dependence on imported industrial inputs meant that a severe foreign exchange constraint on growth developed.

Growing balance-of-payments problems were accompanied by the end of the so-called easy phase of import substitution. By the early 1960s there were few industries where import substitution was not virtually complete. At the same time, macroeconomic policies were extremely expansionary, with the consolidated government budget deficit climbing to 4 percent of GDP by the early 1960s. The accompanying monetary expansion resulted in an acceleration in the rate of inflation, which reached 87 percent in 1964. Coupled with various forms of trade and financial repression, the growing inflation compounded Brazil's economic problems and most likely had a negative effect on output expansion. Slower economic growth, balance-of-payments pressures, accelerating inflation, and growing social unrest all served to contribute towards the military coup of 1964.

The 1968-1974 Economic Boom

While restructuring of political institutions following the 1964 military takeover was fundamental, the changes in economic policy were less dramatic. What changed was not so much the type of economic policies being advocated by policymakers and economists, but the ability to implement such policies.[7] The main thrusts of these economic policy changes were (1) macroeconomic stabilization, in part consisting of the development of better macroeconomic policy instruments, (2) the better use of economic markets for the more efficient allocation of economic resources, and (3) similarly, the partial reorientation of economic policies so as to provide greater incentives to exports.

The myriad of policy reforms adopted in the mid-1960s touched many areas of the economy and included changes in a multitude of specific policy instruments. The reduction of public entity deficits (such as in the railroad system) and revenue-increasing tax reforms did much to lessen the inflationary impact of the government budget. Moreover, the introduction of indexing for financial assets made it easier for the government to finance its deficits in a noninflationary way. In addition to indexation, various other financial reforms served to liberalize financial markets, stimulate their growth, and increase as well the efficacy of government monetary policy.

Similarly, the introduction of a crawling peg exchange rate regime roughly following a basic purchasing power parity rule had the twin effects of simplifying the conduct of monetary policy and reducing uncertainty for exporters. Also originating in the mid-1960s, there was implemented a program of mostly fiscal incentives for manufactured exports by which the real remuneration for exporters was increased. The reduction of a substantial anti-export bias in economic policies was also assisted through a degree of goods markets liberalization. Tariffs were reduced somewhat, and other forms of import liberalization were implemented.

The reorientation of economic policies, involving varying degrees of financial and goods market liberalization, constituted a cautious drawback from the autarchic economic policies of the 1950s toward a more outward-looking economic strategy. These liberalizing, frequently market-oriented policies were soon to pay handsome dividends in terms of restoring high rates of economic growth. As seen in table 1-1, GDP grew at an average of 11 percent annually for the period 1968-1974. To some extent the high growth rates of this period reflect a catching-up-to trend following the slow-growth years of the early 1960s. There was substantial excess capacity by the mid-1960s, so that attaining high rates of output growth was possible with relatively little in the way of investment.[8] At the same time the economic policy changes contributed to both increased domestic savings and the capture of greater amounts of foreign savings—both of which served to increase the growth rate. While the 1968-1974 period is sometimes referred to as the "Brazilian Economic Miracle," what happened during that period was by no means a miracle. Instead, it represented a catching-up from a period in which growth was retarded, and the movement to a higher plane of growth due to the pursuit of growth-inducing economic policies.

The initiation of rapid export growth was one of the noteworthy features of the 1968-1974 boom period. Owing mainly to policy stimuli, exports began growing in the mid-1960s and by 1974 had reached $8.6 billion. This export growth, while still concentrated upon agricultural and primary exports, did much to ease the foreign exchange constraint on Brazilian growth, and in doing so enabled the economy to grow rapidly. The growth in exports also increased Brazil's capacity to borrow abroad, adding further to its resources.

Coping with External Shocks and Slower Growth, 1974-1979[9]

The tentative and cautious opening up of the Brazilian economy was dealt a harsh blow by the petroleum price increases beginning in late 1973. Brazil is dependent upon imported oil for about 80 percent of its petroleum usage, and a drastic increase in its international petroleum bill occurred. Oil imports rose from U.S. $606 million in 1973 (less than 10 percent of total imports) to U.S. $2.6 billion in 1974.[10] A further doubling of the price of oil in 1979 provided a second petroleum shock. By 1979 Brazil found itself importing $3.7 billion of petroleum, and it was expected that the oil bill in 1980 would exceed $9 billion.

The immediate result of the 1973 and 1974 oil price increases was a serious balance-of-payments problem. Going from a slight trade surplus position in 1973, Brazil ran trade deficits in 1974 and 1975 of U.S. $4.7 and $3.5 billion, amounts greater than its total export earnings several years earlier. The terms-of-trade shock and the concomitant balance-of-payments problems presented a policy dilemma to the Brazilian authorities, involving contraction and adjustment to the new international economic situation on the one hand, and temporary expedients, delaying tactics, and autarchic retrenchment on the other. Because of the perceived risks of cutting the ongoing growth process through contractionary macroeconomic policies, the response involved mostly the latter. Two principal measures were employed—the running up of the foreign debt and a dramatic increase in import restrictions.

A reduction in Brazil's international reserves, observed btween 1973 and 1974, was more than complemented by an increase in international borrowing. Brazil's foreign debt, owed mostly to private lenders, grew from U.S. $9.5 billion at the end of 1972 to U.S. $21.1 billion by the end of 1975, and then to a staggering $55 billion by mid-1980.[11] Contracting such indebtedness was facilitated by the high dollar liquidity of the large U.S. and European banks during the 1975 recession and its aftermath. Seen as relative to GDP or exports, the size of Brazil's net international debt has increased markedly. The effect of this borrowing has been to stave off the external adjustment rendered essential by the shocks brought by international economic events.

Brazilian policymakers have also reacted to the balance-of-payments problems associated with the oil price increases by increasing the restrictions on imports. Beginning in 1974 there were widespread tariff increases, with some individual tariff items being increased by 100 percent. The average nominal legal tariff, based upon import weights, was 31.2 percent in 1972 but had risen to 40.6 percent by 1979.[12] More important still than the upward drift of tariff levels since 1973 has been the increase in nontariff barriers. In 1975 an import deposit system was established. The nominal tariff equivalent of this measure has been estimated at a possible 50 percent on the import FOB price for 1978.[13] In January 1979 it was announced that the import deposit system would be gradually phased out, but with the December 1979 economic policy reforms it was eliminated completely. More direct controls over imports also prevail. The tightening up of an elaborate system of controls over imports in the public sector contributed to a reduction of imports by 69 major state enterprises from about U.S. $3 billion in 1975 to $1.8 billion in 1977. In 1979 and 1980 these controls became even more severe with substantial across-the-board cuts imposed on the import budgets of government-owned firms. Outside of the public sector, the ability of firms to obtain tariff exemptions through official incentives programs was made much more difficult. In addition, the importation of a large number of products—particularly finished consumer goods—has been prohibited; import licenses for those goods are simply not granted.

Accompanying the balance-of-payments difficulties in the mid-1970s and the increase in import restrictions was a renewed interest in industrial import substitution as a strategy for Brazilian economic development. Concern about international recession and protectionism in the developed countries coincided with nationalistic sentiments about reducing import dependence. Major government efforts and policy initiatives were mounted in the remaining areas of possible import substitution, namely, basic intermediate inputs and capital goods. Liberal protection for these activities was provided along with heavy doses of subsidized official credit, mostly channeled through the National Development Bank (BNDE) and its affiliates. Large investments in these industries resulted.

The increase in import restrictions, coupled with the slowdown of economic growth, was effective in dampening the growth of imports. As observed in table 1-1, aggregate imports in current U.S. dollars reached a high point in 1974 and then leveled off for the next three years. Non-oil imports were reduced annually until a spurt in 1978. Yet, comparing 1974 non-oil imports with those of 1978, a current dollar reduction of 5 percent is still registered. Taking the significant dollar inflation into account, the reduction in imports becomes all the more dramatic. In addition to their effects on imports, the increased import restrictions have also had an impact on exports through their effect on the allocation of economic resources. The growth of Brazilian exports, along with, quite possibly, the overall growth of the economy, has been slowed by such measures. Reflecting the reduction in the openness of the economy, the proportion of Brazilian GDP accounted for by exports fell 10 percent in 1974 to less than 7 percent by 1978. Had the 1974 international economic shocks been responded to by Brazilian economic policymakers with real exchange-rate depreciation and appropriate macroeconomic policies to reduce absorption, instead of by increasing Brazil's foreign debt and import restrictions, the severe Brazilian balance-of-payments problems arising in the late 1970s would have been much less critical.

In December 1979 the Brazilian government announced a series of economic policy reforms, the central thrust of which was to dismantle some policy-induced distortions and to provide a greater reliance on economic, market signals. A maxidevaluation of the cruzeiro was effected, reducing the nominal value of the cruzeiro by 30 percent. At the same time the fiscal tax credit subsidies for manufacturing exports and the import deposit scheme were eliminated. Steps were also announced to do away with tariff exemptions and rebates, indicating an intention to dismantle a highly discretionary, bureaucratic, and distortionary system of awarding such tariff exemptions. The effect of this particular measure, if effectively pursued, will be to increase the effective cost of imports by placing a greater reliance on legal nominal tariffs, which for the most part are quite substantial. A central question has been whether the essential absorption-reducing and expenditure-switching macroeconomic policy measures necessary to make the devaluation effective have been undertaken. According to the evidence available on the performance of the economy as of mid-1980, it appears that they have not.

The October 1980 Outlook

Macroeconomic policies since mid-1979 have been highly expansionary. Owing to the government budget deficit, the Brazilian monetary authorities have been forced to preside over substantial increases in the money supply. In one month alone (December 1979) the money supply M_1 increased by a full 19 percent. For all of 1979 the federal public sector deficit as a proportion of GDP had reached a very high 7 percent,[14] and it has been necessary to finance this deficitary spending through increases in the money supply. It is clear that such expansionary policies have been responsible for the acceleration in the rate of inflation witnessed between mid-1979 and mid-1980.

While there are numerous reasons for the public sector deficit, three items involving subsidy programs are especially noteworthy. First and most important, agricultural credit for production is an open-ended item in the country's monetary budget, being financed essentially by the government. Since this credit is heavily subsidized (that is, provided at nominal interest rates of about 28 percent annually), the demand for it is, not surprisingly, enormous. Second, the government also maintains a subsidy scheme for domestic wheat production and consumption. It has been reported that the wheat subsidies in 1980 will amount to about Cr \$62 billion (approximately U.S. \$1.1 billion).[15] Finally, there exists a petroleum subsidy program operating through different buying and selling prices as administered through the state monopoly Petrobras. The government has indicated its plans to reduce substantially the wheat and petroleum account subsidies by the end of 1980. Such measures will take considerable pressure off the government budget, but as long as the government maintains a policy of providing unlimited subsidized agricultural credit, the monetary authorities can be expected to have difficulties in restraining the growth of the money supply.

The government's use of indexation has been subjected to progressive undermining since 1975 with the manipulation of the monetary correction coefficients and the exemption of certain forms of credit from "full" monetary correction. In January 1980 the system was effectively scrapped altogether with the announcement of pre-fixed monetary correction coefficients set at 45 percent for the year 1980. In addition, and correspondingly, controls over interest rates in the banking system were extended. The result has been the appearance of heavily negative real interest rates and considerable repression in financial markets. Numerous distortions are evident in such policies, and the growth-rendering longer-term effects of this financial repression may be important.

Accompanying the so-called pre-fixation of the monetary correction coefficients was the concomitant scrapping of the implicit purchasing power parity formula, which guided Brazilian exchange rate policy for the period 1968-1979. It was announced in January 1980 that the nominal exchange depreciation for the year 1980 would be on the order of 40 percent.[16] With inflation proceeding at rates of 100 percent annually, it is clear that such a policy is not sustainable. By June 1980 official IPEA estimates undertaken on a trade-weighted purchasing power parity basis using wholesale prices, put the real exchange rate, including subsidy effects, at a point roughly equal to that which existed prior to the December 1979 maxidevaluation and economic policy reforms. In the absence of policy changes, the resulting increasing overvaluation of the cruzeiro can be expected to exercise prejudicial effects on export performance. Given the magnitude of Brazil's balance-of-payments problems and the necessity to seek new international borrowing, serious questions are raised about the conduct of current exchange rate policy. Not surprisingly, as of this writing (early October 1980) rumors were rife about another maxidevaluation.[17] It is clear that the present exchange rate policy is not sustainable. (In November 1980 the government announced that it would abandon the pre-fixation of both monetary and exchange rate correction as of January 1981.)

The Industrialization of the Economy

As indicated above, the leading sector in Brazilian economic growth in the past thirty years has been industry. The industrial sector has exhibited consistently higher rates of growth than other sectors. By 1979 industrial output accounted for a full 38 percent of Brazilian GDP, as compared to 24 percent in 1950 (table 1-2). It is obvious that with the industrialization of the economy, the importance of agriculture in total output has become reduced. As seen in table 1-2, the output share of the agricultural sector has been reduced continuously; by 1979, it accounted for only 11 percent of GDP.

Table 1-2
Sectoral Shares of GDP, Selected years, 1950-1979
(percent)

Year	*Industry*	*Agriculture*	*Services*
1950	23.5	26.7	49.8
1955	24.4	25.1	50.5
1960	30.3	19.9	50.7
1965	31.8	16.7	51.5
1970	35.4	11.0	53.5
1975	38.1	11.9	50.0
1979	38.1	11.3	50.7

Source: *Conjuntura Econômica,* various issues.

The substantial and continuing growth of the industrial sector has been accompanied by its diversification. Brazil now produces a very wide range of consumer and producer goods. Reflecting this increased industrial diversification is the change over time in the output composition within the manufacturing sector. The share of intermediate and capital goods in total manufacturing output has increased steadily during the last fifty years at the expense of the consumer goods industries. The Textile and Food Processing industries were among the first to be established in Brazil; in 1919, they accounted for 27 and 33 percent of the manufacturing output.[18] Yet, they have been among the slowest growing, as evidenced by the decline of their shares in total manufacturing output to 9 and 21 percent, respectively, in 1977. For the consumer goods industries as a group the decline was from 66 percent to 37 percent between 1949 and 1977. The fastest growing intermediate goods industries were metal products and chemicals: their shares of manufacturing output increased from 8 and 9 percent in 1949 to 16 percent each in 1977. For the capital goods industries the gains have also been dramatic, with substantial gains apparent for machinery, electrical and communications equipment, and transportation equipment. By 1977 these industries accounted for 27 percent of total manufacturing output, as compared to 5 percent in 1949.

The differences in industry growth rates were in great part conditioned by government policies and the import-substituting nature of Brazilian industrialization. The policies accompanying the rapid growth of the Brazilian industrial sector in the postwar period up to 1964 have been described extensively in the literature.[19] The measures taken to promote industrialization included a multiple exchange-rate system affording high levels of protection to some favored industries, while allowing many capital goods imports at highly overvalued exchange rates; substantial credit incentives for industry; fiscal measures designed to lure manufacturing investment into certain regions and types of activities; and, eventually, a restrictive tariff system. The effect of these policies was to foster substantial growth but at the same time to bring about considerable distortions and resource misallocation.

Governmental policies have influenced the pattern of resource usage and investment by differentially affecting profitability in different economic activities. High levels of protection and other policy inducements have favored autarchic industrial development along the lines of forced import substitution. As such, the nature of Brazilian industrialization has been heavily oriented towards the replacement of imports. Several recent studies (Fishlow 1972; Morley and Smith 1970; Tyler 1976) have shown that a major source of Brazilian industrial demand growth until the mid-1960s was import-substituting industrialization. While import substitution was fairly complete for many manufacturing industries by World War II, it has been estimated to have accounted for 24 percent of total manufacturing demand growth in the period 1949-1964 (Tyler 1976). By the mid-1960s, however, import substitution was virtually complete in nearly all manufacturing industries. In 1964 the proportion of imports to available domestic supply for total manufacturing industry was only 6 percent, as compared to 70 percent in 1939 (Tyler 1976). Only in three (admittedly important) industries out of twenty-one did imports in 1964 represent more than 10 percent of total available domestic supply. These three industries—machinery (31 percent), chemicals (11 percent), and miscellaneous manufacturing (13 percent)—still possessed some latitude for continued import substitution. In all others, further import substitution was no longer a viable growth strategy.

During the mid-sixties, and especially after the change of government in 1964, there began a redirection of economic policies which led to a cautious, stop-and-start opening up of the domestic economy.[20] It should be noted, however, that, owing to the relative smallness of manufactured exports in relation to industrial output, export expansion has not yet contributed to total manufacturing demand growth in a major way.[21] In 1974 manufactured exports still accounted for only about 5 percent of total manufacturing output. While this ratio has increased in recent years, its continuing relative smallness indicates that export expansion still does not exercise the predominant influence in accounting for total manufacturing demand growth. The increase in domestic demand has provided the major demand-side impetus for industrial expansion, and its role in any transition from an inward-looking to an outward-oriented industrialization strategy cannot be neglected.

Looking at the process of aggregate and industrial output growth from the supply perspective, technological change in Brazil, as in other countries, has played an important role. Studies employing growth-accounting approaches (Maneschi and Nunes 1970; Langoni 1972), involving the use of an aggregate production function, have attributed large shares of total output growth to technological change. The major work analyzing the importance of technological change in the Brazilian industrial sector has been done by Regis Bonelli (1976). Using a growth-accounting approach and data for the period 1959-1970 for some twenty-one manufacturing industries, he found that 22 percent of the total output growth for all industries could not be explained by either capital stock or labor force increases. This residual was interpreted as representative of technological progress. For some industries—for example, machinery, electrical equipment, and pharmaceutical—the residuals were particularly high. In attempting to explain the interindustry variation in technological change, Bonelli found capital formation particularly important, reflecting capital-embodied technological progress. In any case, policies which have fostered technological improvements and the transfer of technology from the higher-income countries have been conducive to growth.

Efficiency considerations over a period of time are essential for evaluating the efficacy of industrialization policies. Some general indications of increased industrial efficiency in Brazil over the past fifteen years involve: (1) the existence, growth, and variety of Brazilian manufactured exports; (2) the high rates of labor productivity growth in manufacturing, relative to other sectors; (3) an observed increase in the rate of return on capital in the manufacturing sector (Langoni 1971); (4) an apparent decrease in industrial prices relative to other prices (Tyler 1976); and (5) import liberalization and the appearance of widespread redundancy in tariff levels (Bergsman 1970; Tyler 1976). More specific evidence regarding efficiency is available from case studies of individual Brazilian manufacturing industries. Such studies providing evidence that levels of industrial efficiency have increased and reasonable levels of international competitiveness have been attained (given prevailing exchange and fiscal policies) have been done for steel (Baer 1969), some household appliances (Masson 1970), machinery and capital goods (Leff 1968; Vidossich 1974), and some automobile products (Almeida 1972; Bergsman 1970). While not entirely conclusive, this web of evidence suggests that Brazilian industrialization since World War II has not resulted in the implantation of inefficient manufacturing activities. For those industries where postwar industrial growth and import substitution have been the greatest (for example, steel, machinery, and transport equipment) by the late 1970s reasonable international competitiveness had been attained in a large number of lines of production. Protection and autarchic industrial development in Brazil have not led to significant permanent social welfare costs implicit in inefficient manufacturing production. Nor have such protectionistic policies precluded successful export expansion at later stages upon completion of the infancy period.

Industrialization in Brazil has taken place with essentially capitalist socio-economic institutions. In many ways the 1964-1979 Brazilian economic performance and success in attaining high rates of growth were due to the general strategy of (1) fortifying markets and improving the functioning of the price system and (2) increasing the activist role played by the government in the Brazilian economy. Neoclassical policy prescriptions, instrumental in fostering growth, have been skillfully tempered and adroitly applied. With capitalist institutions sound economic policy is not itself sufficient for growth, but conducive, nonstifling policy appears to be a necessary condition. The market mechanism was generally strengthened during this period, and government policies functioned through that mechanism.

The activist role of the Brazilian government in the economy is not inconsistent with the strengthening of markets and the private sector. On the contrary, prevailing governmental economic activity tends to complement rather than compete with the private sector. But governmental influence in the economy is continually growing. In addition to better conceived and more effective economic policy, the government has dramatically increased its directly productive activity through government firms (Baer, Kerstenetsky, and Villela 1973; Tendler 1968; Suzigan 1976). In the manufacturing sector alone government firms in 1979 were estimated to account for 25 percent of total manufacturing sales (Villela and Baer 1980). These firms were concentrated in the high-forward-linkage industries of steel and chemicals. For other sectors such as power, mining, banking, and transportation the government is also the predominant force. In fact, in practically all aspects of organized economic activity in Brazil today, the government exercises a decisive influence through the administration of policies that affect producer profitability in one way or another. To be sure, the present system can be considered one of state capitalism.

While the Brazilian economy has grown rapidly during the postwar period, and especially during the more recent 1968-1974 period, lingering and severe economic problems persist. To a large extent these problems have either been caused or exacerbated by the strategy of economic growth implicitly pursued by the Brazilian authorities through the prevailing constellation of economic policies. Import-substituting industrialization and manufactured export expansion are both strategies of uneven growth. Industrialization is promoted through policy measures concentrating efforts and resources in the industrial sector, generally at the expense of the agricultural sector. Fortunately, in the Brazilian case the discrimination against agriculture has not been so great as to preclude the agricultural sector from registering modest growth. To be sure, growth in the industrial sector has been facilitated by the existence of abundant labor in the agricultural sector and the transfer of some of that labor to the urban areas at low wages. The concentration on industrialization and the administration of development policy have had implications for Brazil's (1) dependence on foreign exchange earnings, (2) allocational efficiency, (3) employment and income distribution, (4) regional income disparities, and (5) heavy reliance on multinational firm operations. Such questions have occupied an important place in the studies and literature dealing with the Brazilian economy. Consequently, these issues and their policy dimensions and implications will be considered in the discussion that follows.

Problems and Issues for Brazilian Industrial Policy

The External Sector and External Indebtedness

One important area of policy attention since the mid-1960s has been the external sector. In the early sixties it became increasingly apparent that a new approach, involving significant departures from prevailing policies, was necessary regarding foreign economic policy in order to end the stagnation of Brazil's exports, in both amount and composition. Import-substituting industrialization, although explicitly a strategy to reduce dependence on the external sector, had not succeeded in significantly reducing the aggregate import-to-GDP ratio. Moreover, the process of industrialization had altered the composition of Brazil's imports, reducing their compressibility, and, if anything, rendering Brazil more dependent on the external sector (Candal et al. 1969). At the same time, Brazil's foreign indebtedness had increased dramatically—to the point where, for the 1962-1966 period, external indebtedness amounted to 22 percent of GDP and 2.4 times annual exports (table 1-3).

As a result of these difficulties, policies were changed to increase the profitability of exports. Among other incentive measures, changes were made in exchange policy, credits for export activities were rendered more accessible, and a series of fiscal incentives for export were instituted (von Doellinger et al. 1973, 1974). The response of these policy measures has been the dramatic export growth witnessed since the mid-1960s. This was particularly the case for the 1965-1974 period. A constant-market-share analysis of Brazilian export performance for a comparable period demonstrates that changes in Brazilian competitiveness, rather than foreign market conditions, accounted for the expansion of exports (Tyler 1976). With the expansion of exports, and of the economy as a whole, the relative magnitude of the external debt diminished, reaching a low in 1973, when the net foreign debt amounted to 7.6 percent of GDP and was equal to 1973 export earnings (table 1-3). During this period, Brazil's international reserves also increased appreciably.

With the balance-of-payments pressures accompanying the external shocks of the mid-1970s, the amount of foreign borrowing was increased substantially. By December 1979 the foreign debt had reached U.S. $49.9 billion.[22] At the same time both GDP growth and export expansion proceeded at lower rates than those during the 1968-1974 boom period. In fact,

Table 1-3
Brazilian External Indebtedness, 1947-1980

Year	Total External Indebtedness (U.S. $ million)	International Reserves (U.S. $ million)	External Indebtedness as a Percentage of GDP: Gross Debt	Net Debt	Ratio of External Debt External Debt to Exports: Gross Debt	Net Debt
1947-1951	590	—	5.2	—	0.47	—
1952-1956	1,227	—	7.7	—	0.83	—
1957-1961	2,201	—	14.5	—	1.67	—
1962-1966	3,545	—	22.3	—	2.39	—
1968	4,310	257	11.6	10.9	2.29	2.15
1969	4,403	656	10.8	9.2	1.91	1.62
1970	5,295	1,187	11.5	8.9	1.93	1.50
1971	6,622	1,723	12.7	9.4	2.28	1.69
1972	9,521	4,183	15.5	8.7	2.39	1.34
1973	12,600	6,417	15.4	7.6	2.03	1.00
1974	17,166	5,269	16.1	10.9	2.16	1.50
1975	21,171	4,041	16.6	13.5	2.44	1.98
1976	25,985	6,544	17.6	13.2	2.57	1.92
1977	32,037	7,256	19.0	14.7	2.64	2.05
1978	43,511	11,895	22.6	16.4	3.44	2.50
1979	49,904	9,682	24.4	19.7	3.27	2.64
1980[a]	57,000	6,000	26.2	23.4	2.78	2.49

Sources: Information for 1947-1966 was reproduced from John T. Donnelly, "External Financing and Short-Term Consequences of External Debt Servicing for Brazilian Economic Development, 1947-1968," *The Journal of Developing Areas,* Vol. 7, No. 3 (April 1973), p. 416. Remaining estimates were calculated from data published in various issues of *Conjuntura Econômica* and *Boletim do Banco Central.*

[a]Author's projections as of September 1980. The 1979 and 1980 estimates were based on 1978 prices and exchange rates.

during the 1974-1978 period Brazilian exports grew more slowly than those of the world as a whole (Tyler 1980). Accordingly, the relevant ratios measuring the relative magnitude of Brazil's external indebtedness have risen, as observed in table 1-3. The running down of international reserves during 1979 and 1980 has compounded difficulties by removing some degrees of freedom for Brazilian policymakers. A key factor in coping with the foreign debt is export growth. With a reduction of export growth rates, obtaining new credits becomes increasingly difficult and costly. Continued export expansion is essential for the Brazilian economy.

Resource Allocation and Industrial Policy

Since World War II, industrialization and industrial growth have been explicit goals of Brazilian policymakers. Policies have been framed to induce industrial growth by pulling available domestic resources into industrial production, and attracting resources from abroad in the form of foreign investment and technology. While these policies have resulted in distortions and some inefficiencies, they have succeeded in bringing about substantial industrial growth (Baer 1965; Bergsman 1970; Lessa 1964; Tavares 1964). While judged inappropriate from a static allocational viewpoint, a strategy promoting industrialization per se in Brazil has not been mistaken when viewed over time. Growth has occurred, factor endowments have changed appreciably, and levels of international competitiveness have been attained in many lines of manufacturing output. To be sure, there has been, and still is, rather widespread productive inefficiency, but the allocational policy decisions in favor of industry as a whole have been correct.

Allocation within the industrial sector is another matter. Industrial policies have not been applied evenhandedly, and the existing industrial structure is in part a reflection of the various incentive measures applied through policy action. Some industries have been favored more than others. Nevertheless, even here there is some evidence to suggest that resource misallocation has not been excessive. In a recent study Bergsman has estimated that the cost of misallocation in the Brazilian manufacturing sector for 1967 amounted to 2 percent of GNP or less (Bergsman 1974).

In discussing resource allocation to and within the Brazilian manufacturing sector, it should be noted that one important characteristic for every Brazilian manufacturing industry is the wide range of productive efficiency exhibited among firms. Some firms produce very efficiently, while others are notoriously inefficient.[23] Cost-minimizing behavior is apparent, but the penalties for not reducing costs are not so noxious. Policies designed to protect or subsidize an entire industry frequently result in large, even monopoly, profits for the efficient firms—and a quiet life free from grave competitive worries for the less efficient firms.

Policies which affect the allocation of resources within the industrial sector can be classified into several broad categories: (1) tariffs and other import restrictions, (2) export incentives, (3) other fiscal measures, (4) credit policy, and (5) government price policy. All of these measures have differential effects across manufacturing industries in Brazil. Moreover, the Brazilian experience illustrates well the Tinbergenian dictum that policies possessing multiple objectives as well as several effects may present conflicts among the objectives. The following discussion concerns the allocational dimensions of each policy category.

Accompanying heavily overvalued exchange rates throughout the last thirty years, high and differing rates of protection have been enjoyed by Brazilian manufacturing industries. As such, exports have been discriminated against. While multiple exchange rates, import quotas, and other protectionist devices such as the Law of the National Similar have been important in protecting Brazilian industry in the past, by the early 1960s tariff policy had emerged as the main policy instrument relied upon for effecting protection. Focusing on tariffs, there have been various attempts to measure the levels of protection afforded to manufacturing industries in Brazil (Bergsman 1970, 1972; Bergsman and Malan 1971; Tyler 1976, 1980a; Neuhaus and Lobato 1978; Savasini et al. 1979; Azambuja et al. 1979). These efforts, summarized in table 1-4, conclude that there exist rather high levels of apparent protection in Brazil. For example, in January 1980 average nominal tariffs, as computed from the tariff schedule, ranged from 23 percent to 203 percent and averaged 101 percent for all manufacturing industries. The interindustry differences in tariff protection indicate a substantial variance in the allocative effects of protection across industries. The range of available tariff protection, and its variability, is even greater at a higher level of disaggregation.

The period 1965-1980 witnessed two distinct and very different phases with respect to import restrictions and tariffs. There was a period of gradual, if halting, import liberalization between 1965 and 1974, followed by a period of increasing import restrictions following 1974. During 1965 and 1966 a substantial loosening up of import restriction was effected through changes in the then-prevailing exchange premium system (Clark 1967). Further liberalization occurred in March 1967 with a general reduction of tariffs and the abolishing of a special, and highly restrictive, category for import (table 1-4). Such liberalization, intensified by a real appreciation of the cruzeiro, proved to be politically unsustainable, and tariffs were revised upwards again in 1968, as indicated in the nominal tariff estimates for January 1969. During the period 1969 to 1974 there was observed a gradual recession of tariff levels for nearly all industries. Between January 1969 and November 1973 the average nominal tariff rate for manufacturing fell from 66 percent to 57 percent. During this period total exports, as well as manufactured exports, were growing rapidly, and the balance-of-payments justifications for heavy import protection were being undermined. Also, the rapid growth of the domestic market made producers less sensitive to import competition.

The general easing downward of tariff levels was also accompanied by a liberalization, and increase, of the tariff exemptions granted to importers under government industrial incentive programs. Especially favored under the tariff exemption schemes were imports of machinery and other capital goods. Reflecting the increased importance of the various tariff exemption programs, the realized tariff rate (that is, actual tariff collections divided by total imports) fell from 12 percent in 1969 to 7 percent in 1974. The effect of all these cautious import liberalization measures was to reduce the bias against export production in the industrial economy, and as a result exports increased markedly.

The pendulum, however, was about to swing back the other way. As has been referred to earlier, tariff levels were increased sharply in the mid-1970s

Table 1-4
Average Rates of Nominal (N) and Effective (E) Tariff Protection for Brazilian Industries, Selected Years
(percent)

	June 1966		April 1967		January 1969	November 1973	January 1980
Industry	*N*	*E*	*N*	*E*	*N*	*N*	*N*[a]
Mining	27	25	14	13	—	22	32
Nonmetallic mineral products	79	86	40	39	51	52	119
Metallurgy	54	58	34	36	47	40	67
Machinery	48	41	34	32	44	38	41
Electrical equipment	114	215	57	97	71	56	80
Transport equipment	108	151	57	75	91	43	106
Lumber and wood	45	45	23	25	67	66	148
Furniture	132	239	68	124	87	76	137
Paper	93	118	48	59	58	49	105
Rubber	101	136	78	116	94	65	119
Leather	108	117	66	85	86	73	125
Chemicals	53	59	34	42	29	22	43
Pharmaceutical products	48	39	37	35	29	21	23
Perfumes, soaps, and so on	192	8,480	94	3,670	29	48	170
Plastics	122	183	81	58	29	44	203
Textiles	181	379	48	162	122	91	164
Apparel	226	337	103	142	176	106	177
Food products	82	87	27	40	40	73	111
Beverages	205	447	83	173	183	131	178
Tobacco	193	313	78	124	167	141	178
Printing	122	142	59	67	44	35	64
Miscellaneous	104	128	58	72	60	42	81
Manufacturing Average	99	181	48	76	66	57	101

Sources: The 1966 and 1967 figures are from Joel Bergsman, *Brazil: Industrialization and Trade Policies* (London: Oxford University Press, 1970), p. 42. Estimates for 1969 are from International Bank for Reconstruction and Development, *Current Economic Position and Prospects of Brazil,* Vol. III Annex 3, *Industrial Policies and the Manufacturing Industries in Brazil* (December 1969). The 1973 estimates are from William G. Tyler, *Manufactured Export Expansion and Industrialization in Brazil* (Tubingen: J.C.B. Mohr, 1976), while estimates for 1980 are from the author's "Recent Effective Tariff Protection for Brazil," *Revista de Estudos Econômicos,* Vol. 10, No. 3 (December 1980), pp. 47-59.

[a]Because of nontariff barriers and widespread tariff redundancy, estimates of effective tariff protection based upon nominal tariffs are highly misleading and are therefore not listed here. Under very strict, and unrealistic, assumptions, the 1980 average available effective rate of tariff protection for manufacturing was estimated at 169 percent.

as a response to balance-of-payment pressures brought on in great part by the petroleum price increases. The increase in tariff levels is demonstrated in table 1-4. Compounding the protective effect of the tariff increases were a number of nontariff import restrictions, briefly described earlier. The system of advance deposits for imports, direct controls on import purchases of government firms, and a tightening up of the tariff exemptions and reductions under industrial programs all had the effect of increasing import restrictions and the protection for domestic production from imports.

It seems clear that export activity in Brazil has been influenced by policies involving import restrictions and their fluctuations. The existence of important restrictions means that prices will be higher in the domestic market than abroad. It therefore becomes more profitable in the absence of other measures to produce for the domestic market than for exports. Economic resources are thus pulled into those sectors receiving protection from import competition and taken from export activities.

Export activities are further hindered by the price-raising effects that protection may have on their intermediate inputs. Protection is rarely selective, and attempts to import-substitute in intermediate goods industries through import restrictions for those goods will have the effect of raising the production costs of all user industries. If the protection provided for the domestic production of intermediate inputs is great, the discrimination against exporters using those inputs can be substantial. Protection from imports of the final products for the input-using industries, while helping in the domestic market, will be of no avail in international markets. Other economic policy instruments must be used to provide offsetting incentives to restore competitiveness and export profitability.

In view of these effects, it is not surprising that the period of import liberalization from 1965 to 1974 was characterized by marked increases in manufactured exports. Through import liberalization and the provision of special export incentives, the anti-export bias of the constellation of Brazilian economic policies was reduced considerably. As a result, exports grew rapidly. Conversely, policy changes during the 1974-1979 period served to increase the anti-export bias for the industrial sector. During this period there was no appreciable change in the export incentives. Consequently, the increase in import restrictions served to increase the profitability of production for the domestic market vis-à-vis that for the export market. Thus, part of the slower growth of Brazilian exports during the 1974-1979 period can be attributed to the increase in import restrictions, a measure which served to brake the rapid export growth of the 1965-1974 period.[24]

The attempts to estimate the effective rates of protection in Brazil have been flawed by a number of features. First, in the earlier studies the level of aggregation, as presented in table 1-4, may be too great to allow making useful generalizations. The availability of a more disaggregated input-output table for the Brazilian economy, based upon the 1970 economic census, has alleviated this problem, and the later studies are much more highly disaggregated. Second, and more important, the measurement of nominal protection in all the available studies is problematic. Economic policies bring about divergences between international and domestic prices for tradeable goods. Tariff policy constitutes but one of these policies. Therefore, to assume, as the available studies do, that tariff levels reflect international-domestic price differences is likely to be inaccurate. This is particularly a problem for the more recent studies, for which periods tariff redundancy and nontariff barriers and incentives have exercised an increased importance.[25]

If there are such problems apparent with the measurement of protection for Brazil, what general conclusion can be drawn from the available studies? First, it is evident that in 1980 the domestic market is heavily protected; the products of many manufacturing industries have been transformed virtually into nontradeables through various economic policies, including tariffs. This protection is frequently excessive, as seen reflected in the nominal available tariffs, exceeding that which could be deemed economically acceptable under infant industry arguments. Many of those industries enjoying the highest tariff protection—nominal or effective—are frequently those which are the oldest and most mature, such as textiles and apparel. Reductions in the levels of protection for such industries would certainly have beneficial effects on allocative efficiency.

A second generalization that can be made from the available studies of protection is that the levels of protection have indeed undergone important changes during the 1965-1980 period, as indicated. The level of protection for manufacturing industries fell considerably between 1966 and 1974. Tariffs were reduced and additional liberalization occurred with the expansion of imports made under tariff-exempted schemes. This liberalization was shortlived, however, and the period since 1974 has seen a return to high levels of protection.

Third, a cascade in the structure of tariff protection has been consistent over time. Consumption goods receive the heaviest tariff protection, followed by intermediate goods and then finally capital goods.[26] Beyond this basic characteristic, which is common in most developing countries, there is no readily identifiable rationale in the structure of protection. No factor of production can be identified as being favored. It almost appears as though the structure of protection is random, worked out haphazardly through producer access and influence in the decision-making process over time. Once imbedded, protective instruments take on an inertia of their own, making it very difficult to remove them despite changing circumstances.

The existence of a considerable anti-export bias in the impact of economic policies is suggested by the studies of protection. Yet, the magnitude of any anti-export biases for industries depends not only on import restrictions, but on other policies as well affecting divergences between domestic and international prices. Export incentives are of crucial importance, since they can allow a producer to compete in international markets despite heavy protection in the domestic market. Since the mid-1960s Brazil has employed a number of special incentives for export, involving fiscal and credit schemes. Looking first at the fiscal measures, the fiscal incentives for export have included: (1) exemption from the federal industrial product tax (the IPI, for Imposto de Produtos Industrializados) for exports, (2) a tax credit based upon the IPI for products exported, (3) exemption from the state value added taxes (the ICM, for Imposto de Circulaçao de Mercadorias) for exports, (4) a tax credit based on the ICM for exports, (5) an income tax exemption for profits earned from exports, (6) exemption from the payment of various minor taxes for products exported, and (7) drawback provisions allowing duty-free import of goods used to produce final product exports. With the exception of the drawback incentives, the receipt of the fiscal incentives for an exporting firm is automatic. There is no room under the regulations for a discretionary awarding of the fiscal incentives on a case-by-case basis. All firms exporting manufactured products receive the fiscal incentives.

The use of the IP and ICM tax credits constituted a pure subsidy element in the export incentives. In 1977 these subsidies averaged 18.6 percent of the *ex factory* price for manufacturing exporters.[27] Once in place there was little change in these incentives over time, but the implementation of the various fiscal incentives did have a highly beneficial effect on the real remuneration of exporters. In fact, while exchange-rate policy for the period 1968-1979 stabilized real exporter remuneration, the implementation of the fiscal incentives served as the means by which such remuneration was increased.

In addition to affecting overall exporter remuneration for manufactured exports, the fiscal incentives have raised allocative questions. The IPI tax rates, instrumental in determining the quantitative magnitude of the fiscal incentives, differ from product to product. As a result, the export subsidies have differed across products and industries. A question that then arises is how rational is the structure of the incentives in view of Brazil's presumed international comparative advantage in more labor-intensive (that is, unskilled labor) products? In comparing the overall efficiency of exchange-rate policy versus fiscal policy in increasing local currency remuneration per unit of foreign exchange earned through exports, economic theory provides no immediate answer. However, if the fiscal subsidies are not applied uniformly at the same level to all products, differing fiscal subsidies can contribute to allocational inefficiency. Clearly, uniform fiscal subsidies are superior to differing fiscal subsidies on theoretical grounds. The question of allocational inefficiency through export expansion policies arises only when subsidies are involved. The exemption of taxes for exported products affects all products uniformly, and involves subsidy elements only to the extent that public goods are used in the production process.

Because of the variation of the IPI tax rates over products, the fiscal subsidies for export have also displayed considerable differences across products and industries. The combined fiscal subsidy rates for exports for the IPI and ICM subsidy mechanisms ranged from −7.9 percent (an export tax) to 35.5 percent in 1977, although many industries were clustered in the 20-30 percent range (appendix table A-2). Such substantial variations in the rate of nominal export subsidies possess important allocational implications.[28] With the December 1979 economic policy reforms the purely fiscal export subsidies, based upon the IPI and ICM tax credits, were eliminated, thereby greatly reducing the interindustry variation in the export incentives. The remaining export incentive instruments, while not possessing the quantitative magnitude of the eliminated fiscal subsidies, still do vary over industries. The most important of these is the subsidized credit mechanism for export production. The value of these subsidies averaged 5 percent, on a value-of-product basis, for 1977. Yet, over industries they varied from zero to 13.7 percent (appendix table A-2).

In addition to the allocative aspects of the fiscal incentives for export, other tax policies also have allocative effects. Given the structure of domestic demand, differing product taxes (the IPI) affect the allocation of resources for domestic production. *Ceteris paribus*, resources are pulled to those industries with the lowest taxes. Net allocational criteria are not paramount in determining the structure of the product tax system. There are some suggestions that equity considerations are taken into account, and revenue considerations also appear to be important, as evidenced by the high taxes on cigarettes and alcoholic beverages.

Numerous fiscal incentive programs have been established for industrial promotion as a whole. In addition to the fiscal incentives for exports, these programs have included: (1) tariff reductions for the importation of certain capital goods and intermediate products for government-approved projects, (2) special fiscal credits provided to the steel industry, and (3) IPI exemptions and credits for the domestic capital goods industry. Although it is not possible to discern in any great detail the value of these incentives on an industry basis, the total amount, that is, the fiscal cost, of all these incentives awarded to manufacturing industries in 1979 was Cr $115.5 billion (roughly U.S. $4.5 billion), equal to approximately 8.7 percent of total manufacturing output for that year.[29]

Allocational effects are also apparent through the application of credit policy. Many subsidized credit schemes exist in Brazil, and their administration tends to be uneven across manufacturing industries (Suzigan et al. 1972). The data collected and made available by the various financial institutions in Brazil do not lend themselves to a quantitative assessment of the discriminatory impact of credit policy on an industry basis. The overall effect, however, while varying over time, appears to have been substantial.

Summing up the credits provided to industry in 1979 in the form of financing provided through the BNDE system, the Banco do Brasil, and the commercial banking system, it has been estimated that the absolute amounts of the credit subsidies for industry in 1978 and 1979 were Cr $37.2 billion and Cr $164.8 billion, respectively. The 1979 industrial credit subsidy was thus roughly equivalent to U.S. $6.4 billion and approximately equal to 12.4 percent of manufacturing output, as compared to 4.7 percent for 1978.[30] Owing to an increase in financial repression and the rate of inflation, the credit subsidies in 1980 will undoubtedly continue to grow in real terms.

Government price controls and pricing policy also have an important impact on the interindustry allocation of resources. To the extent that domestic industrial prices are controlled by the government and maintained at lower than free market, that is, uncontrolled, prices, disincentives are apparent. Since price controls are likely not to be uniformly applied across sectors, relative prices are likely to be distorted.

While there is a long experience of attempts in Brazil to control prices, the present institutional apparatus dates from December 1967 with the establishment of the Interministerial Price Council (CIP). Under present arrangements the CIP exercises vast authority in the setting of industrial prices. In 1976 some 4,200 manufacturing firms were subject to examination and price controls on the part of CIP; these firms accounted for about 43 percent of Brazil's total manufacturing output during that year.[31] Since then, CIP's influence and scope of operations have been increased.

For most of its existence CIP has exercised a rather passive role, passing on cost increases for those firms subject to price controls. Its ostensible criterion for granting price increases has revolved around the maintenance of firm profitability in the face of documented cost increases. During the 1976-1978 period the prices for CIP-controlled firms and products increased slightly less than for comparable uncontrolled firms and products (de Mata 1980). However, some marked interindustry differences could be observed, suggesting distortions in relative prices. Some industries, including most notably pharmaceuticals and chemical products, appear to have been adversely affected in that the controlled prices increased significantly less than the uncontrolled prices for those industries. It would appear that the industries most subjected to vigorous CIP price controls are those characterized by oligopolistic market structures, substantial forward linkages, and foreign firm participation.

Beginning in early 1979 efforts have been undertaken to alter the role of CIP to one of greater activism in controlling prices. The objective of the government in using the CIP in this fashion has been to diminish the rate of inflation through the squeezing of prices subject to control. A similar strategy was employed during the 1972-1973 period. Whether this effort will be successful in any more than the fairly short run is open to considerable doubt. Moreover, the costs in undermining the economic formation of prices are likely to be great. After one year of increasing CIP severity there was evidence apparent that relative prices were being considerably distorted. Firms were complaining vociferously, and charges of abuse were frequently heard. Moreover, various black markets for controlled products had developed. For one product—cement—for which prices for the past few years have been tightly controlled, reinvestment in the industry has evidently—and predictably—been adversely affected. After years of self-sufficiency, and even exportation, Brazil is expected to become once again a net importer of cement in 1981.

Employment and Income Distribution

Without question Brazil's most pressing socio-economic problem is the underutilization of labor and the concomitant unequal distribution of income. The problem of poverty and the lack of job opportunities is most readily apparent in the urban sector. Underemployment in the cities has reached dramatically high levels. One study has estimated that for 1968 visible underemployment (those unwillingly working less than 40 hours weekly) and disguised unemployment (arbitrarily defined as those earning less than roughly $13 per month) constituted 30 percent of the Brazilian nonrural labor force (O'Brien and Salm 1970). For its part, the industrial sector has been conspicuously unable to absorb large increases in the labor force despite rapid industrial growth. By 1970, after years of rapid industrial growth, only 8.7 percent of the labor force was engaged in industry. For the entire period 1949-1974 manufacturing employment increased by only 4.4 percent annually, absorbing only a minor part of a large labor surplus (de Mata 1978). If ever import-substituting industrialization was thought by its proponents to resolve the unemployment problem in Brazil, it must be judged a failure. Even in the eyes of the most ardent advocates of import-substituting industrialization (see, for example, Tavares 1964), its employment performance has been clearly less than satisfactory. In our view, the economic policies adopted in conjunction with the import-substituting effort bear a major responsibility in contributing to the employment and surplus labor problem.

The failure of import-substituting industrialization (ISI) to absorb labor sufficiently in industrial employment in Brazil, and in other developing countries, has been attributed to a number of reasons, and something of a controversy has developed between, as one writer has succinctly expressed it, the "structural" critics and the "market" critics of ISI (Baer 1972). In Brazil, manufacturing growth has been greatest in those industries that are the most capital-intensive. In other words, the product mix accompanying

Brazilian industrialization has been concentrated, at least in recent times, in those industries providing the least direct employment generation. In addition, disregarding the product mix, there are problems of absorbing labor within given industries, and this is where the greatest controversy lies. Stressing the capital-intensive character of ISI, the structuralist critics argue that labor absorption has been low because of limited possibilities for factor substitution, the importance of foreign firms and their tendency to utilize production techniques existing in the home country, the inclination of domestic producers also to copy techniques existing in the developed countries, the capital-using bias in technological change, and the absence of technology appropriate for the factor endowments of the less-developed countries (Eckaus 1935; Baer and Hervé 1966; Furtado 1968). For the "structural" critics, relative factor prices are of little importance. Seen in this fashion, wage policy is primarily a distributive instrument.

The market-critic interpretation, on the other hand, stresses the importance of relative factor prices in determining the amounts of different factors employed. This line of reason argues that without the severe distortions introduced into the factor markets by government policy, the labor absorption problem would be far less, or perhaps even nonexistent. Credit, fiscal, and exchange incentives have been liberally extended in Brazil to promote investment in the industrial sector. These measures have had the effect of rendering the private price of capital cheap relative to its social opportunity cost. In the labor market, on the other hand, government measures have had the effect of rendering the private price of capital cheap relative to its social opportunity cost. In the labor market, on the other hand, government measures have served to increase the price of labor to a level greater than its social opportunity cost. An elaborate system of social welfare and labor legislation in Brazil, dating back to the Vargas period, has included such features as minimum wage laws, liberal vacation pay, a Christmas bonus equal to one month's pay, severance pay depending upon time of service, and a wide range of other fringe benefits. One study has estimated that in 1971 the various fringe benefits to labor increased the employer's cost of unskilled labor by 42 percent in relation to the minimum wage (Bacha et al. 1972). The combined effect of the capital and labor market distortions has been to increase substantially the relative prices of labor, thereby resulting in more capital-intensive methods of production.

Which of the two different interpretations is correct is an empirical question of considerable policy significance, which has not yet been adequately resolved by empirical analysis. There is some evidence supporting both interpretations, suggesting some elements of accuracy in both. Ultimately, however, the empirical resolution of the controversy concerning labor absorption lies in determining the importance of relative factor prices in the employment of those productive factors. In other words, to what degree does factor substitutability exist? Through analysis based upon interviews with managers of selected manufacturing firms in Brazil, Morley and Smith (1974) have presented evidence which provides a pessimistic picture as to the scope for possible factor substitution. On the other hand, the available econometric estimates of production functions indicate reasonably high observed elasticities of substitution for Brazilian manufacturing industries (Goodman et al. 1971; Tolosa 1974; Tyler 1974).

If we are to confide at all in the latter studies, which find the scope of factor substitution far greater than that argued by the structuralist critics, it must be concluded that ISI-associated economic policies, subsidizing capital and otherwise altering relative factor prices, must bear much of the blame in contributing to Brazil's current underemployment situation. One cannot help but wonder what would have been the outcome if, instead of subsidizing the use of capital, government policy had subsidized the use of labor in the attempt to promote industrialization. The implications of such an alternative strategy are indeed great, both for the product mix and the distribution of income. To have pursued such a policy, however, would have required an entirely different constellation of political power.

One of the consequences of low labor absorption in industry and high rates of underemployment is the lopsided distribution of income prevailing in Brazil. The availability of the 1970 Demographic Census data has led to a spate of studies of the distribution of income, and particularly of how income distribution changed since the earlier comparable census year of 1960 (for example, Fishlow 1971; Hoffman and Duarte 1972; Langoni 1972). These studies all demonstrate an increase in distributional inequality between 1960 and 1970, although they differ widely in their interpretation as to the explanatory factors. It is clear, however, that the gains from the rapid economic growth occurring during the period were very unevenly distributed. While absolute income levels of the poorest elements of the population were essentially unchanged, dramatic increases in real incomes were enjoyed by the middle and upper income group.

In addition to these essentially descriptive studies, the relationship between economic growth, industrial structure, and the distribution of income has been explored in a number of studies using closed-loop input-output models of the Brazilian economy (Cline 1972; Lopes 1972; Morley and Smith 1973; Morley and Williamson 1974). By and large, these latter studies have concluded that a progressive redistribution of income would have little effect on the aggregate rate of growth. What would happen to the composition of output is another story. While Morley and Smith indicate little change in production structure, Lopes rather convincingly argues that the effect of progressive redistribution on the composition of final demand would over time significantly change the composition of Brazilian output. He finds that a movement towards equalization would increase the growth rate for agriculture, commerce, services, perfumery, textiles, apparel, leather, food products, beverages, and tobacco. On the other hand, the economy's so-called "dynamic" sectors would witness slower rates of growth especially in transport equipment, petroleum products, rubber, and electrical equipment. In other words, the observed "dynamics" of certain industries and the rates of industrial growth in Brazil are concluded to be intricately related to the distribution of income. Therefore, policies affecting the income distribution must also be considered in view of their effects on the pattern of industrial growth. Likewise, the converse could be argued.

Regional Income Disparities

Another focus on the subject of income distribution in Brazil is to consider the regional distribution of income. While regional conflict, conciliation, and compromise have been major shaping forces in postcolonial Brazilian history, it has not been until the twentieth century that regional income disparities have become accentuated and politically objectionable. Brazil's populous Northeast, containing 30 percent of the total Brazilian population in 1970, has not kept up with the country's industrial growth. The industrial spurt has occurred in the Brazilian Center-South, most notably in the state of São Paulo. Rapid growth in the Center-South, spurred by industrial expansion in conjunction with the Northeast's failure to respond to changing demand conditions in international agricultural markets, has eroded the relative position of the Northeast. Although it accounted for about 17 percent of total Brazilian income in 1939, the Northeast's share had fallen to 12 percent by 1970. The per capita income disparity has also increased. In 1939 the Northeast's per capita income was about 48 percent of the average Brazilian per capita income, but by 1975 it had fallen to 44 percent (Cavalcanti and Cavalcanti 1976; Tyler 1976). The decline would have been more pronounced had it not been for (1) the substantial emigration from the Northeast to the more industrialized Center-South and (2) government policy promoting investment in the Northeast.[32]

The incentives offered for investment in the Northeast have been responsible for the initiation of much industrial enterprise in the region (Goodman and Cavalcanti 1971, 1974; Suzigan et al., 1974). Financing has been made available through SUDENE and the Bank of the Northeast under an involved tax credit scheme known as Article 34/18.[33] After deposit under the plan, the 34/18 funds are made available to investors for industrial projects in the Northeast at subsidized interest rates. Between January 1962 and April 1970 SUDENE approved 581 industrial projects in the Northeast totaling U.S. $1.4 billion in 1960 prices (Goodman and Cavalcanti 1974). The result of the investment carried out under the auspices of Article 34/18 and the Bank of the Northeast has been to stimulate industrial growth. Manufacturing output grew at an annual rate of 5.0 and 4.4 percent annually during the respective 1949-1959 and 1959-1965 periods. However, during the 1966-1974 period, when 34/18 projects were beginning to come into operation, industrial output grew at 8.7 percent annually.[34]

There are two noteworthy effects apparent with the SUDENE incentives. First, there is a bias in the structure of the incentives that discriminates in favor of import-substituting activities (such as capital and intermediate goods) and against export activities. An elaborate rating system exists, awarding points for different features of an investment project. The higher the total points amassed, the more 34/18 financing is available. Analyzing the totality of the point system, the existing SUDENE investment incentives appear to possess a latent bias against the development of export-oriented manufacturing industry. Second, the incentive system operates primarily through a subsidy for capital investment. As such, not only are capital-intensive industries favored more, but more capital-intensive methods within each industry are promoted. As a result, it has been observed that the industrial growth of the Northeast has been heavily capital-intensive (Goodman and Cavalcanti 1974).

Some efforts have been made to learn from these experiences in the Northeast for development programs in other low-income Brazilian regions, such as Amazonia and the Center-West. In the Amazon region, for example, while there exist incentives for industrial investment as well as other forms of investment, the greatest impetus has been in large-scale agricultural projects, particularly cattle ranching (Mahar 1979). Looking on the incentives as a whole, there is lacking a comprehensive and integrated scheme of incentives for regional development. Moreover, relatively little research has been carried out to study the regional income transfers effected in Brazil through the 34/18 mechanism, the state value added tax, the industrial product tax, government expenditures, and the channeling of subsidized credits.[35] In fact, the whole question of the overall spacial impact of economic policies, both spacial and nonspacial, is one which has been little studied in Brazil. It seems obvious, for example, that industrialization policies, involving protection to domestic manufacturing industries and exchange-rate overvaluation, have served to discriminate against the poorer regions. Whether the magnitude of the implicit negative subsidies for these regions under such policies has been overcome by subsidies deriving from explicit regional development programs remains an open question.

Foreign Investment and Multinational Firms

One of the characteristics of post-World War II Brazilian industrialization has been its reliance on foreign investment and multinational firms. During this period the foreign presence in the economy has grown markedly, especially in the manufacturing sector. In the make-up of overall postwar Brazilian industrialization strategy, if indeed one consciously existed, the foreign firm was to exercise an important role. With the relative debility of domestic private manufacturing enterprise, rapid industrial expansion came to rely heavily upon foreign enterprise for capital, technology, and entrepreneurship. Inviting foreign firms in and providing a hospitable and profitable environment created an opportunity to close the perceived gap between immediate domestic capabilities and the requirements of rapid industrialization, especially in those nontraditional industries where investments were large and lumpy, and technical requirements great. The heavy protection afforded to Brazilian industries, in addition to promoting those industries, had the effect of attracting foreign investment which otherwise would not have located in Brazil.

The extent of foreign capital penetration in the Brazilian economy has generated considerable controversy by economists and others at various levels of sophistication.[36] Foreign capital entering Brazil is required by law to be registered with the Central Bank, as are reinvestments of earnings by foreign firms. According to the Central Bank information, registered foreign capital in Brazil totaled U.S. $14.5 billion as of June of 1979, with 77 percent invested in manufacturing.[37] However, because of inadequate accounting procedures this figure seriously understates foreign investment in Brazil. One study (Tyler 1977) estimated that in 1971 the shares of total manufacturing net assets controlled by government firms, foreign firms, and privately owned domestic firms were 18.5, 34.4, and 47.1 percent, respectively. For all industry, government firms were concentrated and most important in mining, iron and steel, petrochemicals, and petroleum refining and distribution. Foreign firms had a share of the assets in nearly all manufacturing activities. The greatest concentrations of foreign enterprise were to be found in tobacco (98 percent), machinery (68 percent), rubber (67 percent), electrical equipment (65 percent), pharmaceutical products (61 percent), and transportation equipment (57 percent). While based upon similar but less complete data coverage, estimates of the market shares for foreign firms provide similar, but slightly higher percentages. Moreover, when the 1971 estimates are compared with those of earlier studies (Jaspersen 1970; Morley and Smith 1971), it is apparent that the foreign firm share, as well as that for government firms, has risen. Given the observed market share increase and output growth, it is estimated that foreign firms have accounted for about 60 percent of the increase in manufacturing production between 1965 and 1971.

Ultimately, the question of foreign firm participation in the domestic economy is one of control. To what extent does the existence and operation of multinational firms in Brazil provide problems of policy effectiveness and control for the Brazilian authorities? Short-run destabilizing effects may well exist with respect to exchange and monetary policy. Capital flight is always a potentiality, but it should be remembered that government policy is capable of response. In a sense, the foreign capital presence constitutes a hostage in the hands of the Brazilian government both with respect to economic policy and political ends. Moreover, the thought that foreign firms are strong enough and sufficiently united to dictate amenable economic policy to an administratively capable, competent, and strong government is naive. Foreign firms have interests similar to those of nationally owned private-sector firms, and they respond in much the same manner to policy measures. Certainly, the argument that foreign firms exercise undue influence in the LDC policy formulation is mitigated in the case of a powerful, far-reaching, and effective government. Such is the case with Brazil, where the government has emerged as the dominant single force in the economy.[38] Estimates of the total governmental share of GDP range up to 50 percent, and by 1969 the public sector accounted for about 61 percent of total investment (Baer, Kerstenetsky, and Villela 1973). With a perceived weakness in the domestic private sector, the choice for a development-minded government intent on large amounts of growth in a hurry is between foreign and government productive activity. The Brazilian government has chosen both alternatives, with the period since 1964 witnessing a progressive strengthening of governmental control over the economy.

Notes

1. World Bank, *World Development Report, 1980*, August 1980, p. 115.

2. Ibid., p. 111.

3. Fundação Instituto Brasileiro de Geografia e Estatística, *Pesquisa Nacional por Amostra de Domicílios*, 1977.

4. Knight et al., *Brazil: Human Resources Special Report* (Washington: The World Bank, October 1979), Annex 3, pp. 64-65. These estimates were based upon ENDEF data.

5. William G. Tyler, *Manufactured Export Expansion and Industrialization in Brazil* (Tubingen: J.C.B. Mohr, 1976), p. 68.

6. Alexander Gerschenkron, *Economic Backwardness in Historical Perspective* (Cambridge, Mass.: Harvard University Press, 1962).

7. For a discussion see the introductory chapter in Rosenbaum and Tyler (1972).

8. The incremental capital-output ratio for the 1967-1968 period had risen to 4.1, as contrasted to 2.2 for the 1948-1962 period. During the boom period it fell to very low levels; for 1968-1972 an incremental capital-output ratio of 1.6 was estimated (Tyler 1976, p. 290).

9. This section draws heavily on the author's *Advanced Developing Countries as Export Competitors in Third World Markets: The Brazilian*

Experience, Significant Issues Series, 2, no. 8 (Washington: Center for Strategic and International Studies of Georgetown University, 1980), pp. 12-15.

10. Banco do Brasil, *Comércio Exterior: Séries Estatísticas*, 1978, p. 1. In comparison, total petroleum imports in 1968 amounted to only U.S. $138 million.

11. *Boletim do Banco Central*, various issues.

12. Author's calculations based upon CIEF information. These estimates exclude petroleum imports, which are duty-free. A simple unweighted average, calculated from the tariff schedules, rose from 58 percent in 1975 to 81.6 percent in 1977. See Joal de Azambuja Rosa et al., "Alguns Aspectos da Política Tarifária Recente," Fundação Centro de Estudos do Comércio Exterior, unpublished paper, November 1979, pp. 19-20.

13. For a discussion of this and other similar instruments, see chapter 2. Because of exemptions the actual weight felt from the import deposit is less than its possible tariff equivalent. The realized tariff equivalent of the import deposit for 1977 was estimated to be 16.2 percent. See Azambuja (1979).

14. IPEA, *Relatório Trimestral*, January-March 1980, p. 28. For 1980 it was projected that the comparable figure would be around 5 percent.

15. *Jornal do Brasil*, August 11, 1980, p. 15.

16. In part to gain more time the government subsequently announced that the relevant period would be July 1980-June 1981, for which the nominal depreciation was set at approximately 50 percent.

17. In late September the U.S. dollar was selling in the parallel (that is, black) market at a premium of 25 percent over the official rate.

18. See appendix table A-1. For the development and presentation of the 1977 data see Regis Bonelli and Dorothea Werneck, "Desempenho Industrial: Auge e Desaceleração nos Anos 70," in *Indústria: Política, Instituições e Desenvolvimento*, Wilson Suzigan, ed. Monograph no. 28 (Rio de Janeiro: INPES/IPEA, 1979), p. 190.

19. For two good analyses of postwar industrialization policies see Werner Baer, *Industrialization and Economic Development in Brazil* (Homewood, Illinois: Richard D. Irwin, 1965) and Joel Bergsman, *Brazil: Industrialization and Trade Policies* (London: Oxford University Press, 1970).

20. Consequently, the contribution of import substitution to total manufacturing demand growth for the period 1964-1971, as measured proportionally, was estimated as negative (Tyler 1976).

21. About 6 percent of total manufacturing demand growth in the period 1967-1971 was accounted for by export expansion (Tyler 1976).

22. One important but frequently disregarded advantage in accumulating such a large foreign debt is that these loans are very cheap.

While most of the debt is private, such borrowing, through the euro-currency markets, has been done at negative real interest rates.

23. Some econometric evidence is available in Tyler (1979) and Lee and Tyler (1978).

24. Some empirical evidence of the effects of changes of the anti-export bias on Brazilian export performance is contained in Tyler (1980b).

25. Two of the more recent studies (Neuhaus and Lobato 1977 and Savasini et al. 1979) try to avoid the serious redundancy problems by using realized tariffs as their measure of nominal protection. We feel, however, that this procedure is inappropriate, as is explained in appendix B.

26. With the 1980 nominal tariff rates the averages are as follows: consumption goods, 140 percent; intermediate goods, 93 percent; and capital goods, 67 percent (Tyler 1980a). This basic cascade also appears in all other studies for both nominal and effective tariff protection.

27. See appendix table A-2.

28. See Savasini (1978) and Savasini et al. (1979).

29. Suzigan (1980), p. 3. Data are from INOR/IPEA. This total amount cannot properly be considered as a production subsidy to manufacturing, as nearly one-half of the total (CR $70.7 billion) consisted of tariff reductions and exemptions for approved industrial projects.

30. Ibid, p. 15.

31. For the best treatment of industrial price controls in Brazil, see da Mata (1980). For an earlier analysis see Carneiro (1976).

32. The rationale for regional industrial policies is discussed in Lodder (1978). For an overview of regional development patterns see Baer and Geiger (1978).

33. SUDENE is the Superintendency for the Development of the Northeast (Superintendência do Desenvolvimento do Nordeste).

34. See Goodman and Cavalcanti (1974) for a good discussion of the 34/18 incentives and an analysis of their effects on industrial output.

35. Notable exceptions are the studies by Rezende and Silva (1974) and Rebouças et al. (1979).

36. Some of the more useful analyses include Jaspersen (1970), Pignaton (1973), Morley and Smith (1971), von Doellinger and Cavalcanti (1975), Suzigan (1976), Evans (1979), and Villela and Baer (1980).

37. *Boletin do Banco Central*, 16, no. 2 (February 1980), pp. 196-201.

38. For a good analysis see Suzigan (1976).

2 Industrial Promotion and Incentives: The Capital-Goods Sector, 1975-1979

Introduction

The observed growth of the Brazilian capital-goods sector has been affected by economic policy. In Brazil, as in other countries, industrial policy affects the relative profitability of certain industries vis-à-vis other industries, and that of manufacturing as a whole in relation to other sectors of the economy. Since the government is involved in very few directly productive activities in the capital goods sector, profitability must serve as the economic lure to attract resources to the sector. Government policies affect the profitability of different economic activities primarily through their effects on relative prices, as seen through two dimensions. Prices of a Brazilian tradable product, in our case a capital good, relative to international prices and relative to the prices of other Brazilian products, are both important and affected by economic policies. The prices of all Brazilian tradable goods vis-à-vis Brazilian nontradables are affected by the management of exchange-rate policy, which likewise affects the overall international competitiveness of Brazilian tradables. In addition, other economic policies affect the relative prices of products within Brazil. The analysis of this chapter focuses on the possible differences between international and domestic prices, given the application, sometimes administered quite discretionarily, of different economic policy instruments.

While implemented by different agencies and levels of government for widely differing objectives, there are basically five areas of policy that affect the profitability and competitiveness of the Brazilian capital goods industry. They are: exchange-rate policy, import restrictions on capital goods, tax incentives to domestic producers and users of capital goods, financial incentives and subsidies, and protection of the domestic industries supplying inputs to the Brazilian capital-goods industry.

Each of these policy areas will be discussed separately.[1] Subsequently, an attempt will be made to assess the overall quantitative impact of these policies. The overall question is the extent to which the Brazilian capital-goods industry is protected and promoted as a consequence of economic policy. Accordingly, a system of measuring net protection is developed

This chapter was published in Portuguese as "Restrições à Importação e Incentivos Fiscais papa o Setor de Bens de Capital no Brasil: 1975/79," *Pesquisa e Planejamento Econômico* 10, no. 2 (August 1980). Reprinted with permission.

and applied to conditions existing in 1978-1979. Changes in the policy environment taking place with the economic policy reforms announced in December 1979 are not included.[2] A final section will make some observations on the competitiveness of the Brazilian capital-goods sector.

Exchange-Rate Policy

Exchange-rate policy has been pursued in Brazil for a number of objectives not related to industrial development. The exchange rate prevailing during the 1975-1979 period was heavily overvalued, and as such it discriminated against the export sector and, *ceteris paribus*, against import-substituting sectors. Estimates vary as to the extent of the exchange-rate overvaluation but generally are in the 25 to 35 percent range.[3] These estimates are necessarily rather crude, involving, as they must, assumptions about capital flows, changes in other policies, tariff and trade restrictions external to Brazil, and price elasticities.

Changes in exchange-rate policy over time can affect the degree of overvaluation. Yet, in recent years there has been little change in the administration of exchange-rate policy. The expressed government policy is to devalue the currency regularly in accordance with domestic inflation and inflation in Brazil's major trading partners. The objective has been to maintain the real purchasing power parity for the currency. A recent analysis of Brazil's exchange-rate movements indicates that the real exchange rate, adjusted for domestic and international inflation, did not undergo substantial change in the 1973-1979 period.[4] There has been observed a slight decline in the purchasing parity exchange-rate index, indicating that the cruzeiro has been gradually depreciated in terms of other currencies. This real depreciation has not been dramatic, and, in fact, may be somewhat overstated by the use of later year trade weights. Moreover, because of the important exogenous increase in petroleum import prices, one can argue that the rate of exchange-rate depreciation should have been greater. This view is suggested by the fact that import restrictions since the mid-1970s have increased. Nonetheless, the degree of exchange-rate overvaluation is unlikely to have changed appreciably during the 1975-1979 period. As such, changes in exchange-rate policy during these years were not significant in *altering* the relative profitability and competitiveness of the Brazilian capital-goods sector.

Import Restrictions

Import restrictions per se incorporate both tariff and nontariff barriers. Since they are more visible and more readily quantifiable, much of the attention devoted to Brazilian trade restrictions has focused on tariffs. Yet, tariffs, while significant, are not the principal form of restriction on imports in Brazil. An import deposit scheme, some direct import restrictions for government enterprises, a national-origin preference for government purchases, and an involved system of fiscal incentives all serve to restrict the imports of capital goods, as well as of other products. Similarly, the effects domestically are to increase domestic prices and output levels. When considered together, the indirect controls on imports constitute an implicit quota system. The determination of what can be imported, however, as will be discussed below, is not unrelated to the tariff levels. While it would have been desirable to have made direct price comparisons to assess quantitatively the impact of Brazil's import restrictions, such implicit tariff calculations, on a meaningful basis, have been precluded by the unavailability of suitable data. Tariffs on capital goods range from 7 to 205 percent. The extremes, however, are limited in importance. Tariffs on the most common types of equipment fall in the 35 to 55 percent range. A simple arithmetic mean for nominal tariff rates on capital goods for all such products listed in the tariff schedule was 45.8 percent in 1974.[5] Weighting the average for the same year by imports produced a mean of 40.8 percent. There were growing balance-of-payments pressures in 1974-1975, and consequently there has been some upward adjustment in tariff levels. Most of these adjustments occurred in 1975. By 1977 the import-weighted tariff average was 46.6 percent for all capital goods, as seen in table 2-1. The tariff increases appear more pronounced if the year 1972 (before the 1973 oil crisis) is used as a reference point. Table 2-2 presents a comparison between 1972 and 1978 tariff levels for the six major capital goods items in the Brazilian trade classification (NBM). As seen, all categories witnessed increases in nominal tariffs except the low-nominal-tariff Shipbuilding group. Estimations similar to those made in table 2-2 for 1976 demonstrated few changes in the import-weighted nominal tariffs between 1976 and 1978.

A similar picture of increased tariff protection is presented by the observed changes in realized tariffs. As will be shown in a discussion to follow, tariff exemptions and reductions are common features in Brazilian commercial and industrial policy. These reductions are reflected in the realized tariff rates, which are computed by dividing tariff revenues actually collected by imports. Table 2-2 demonstrates that in all but one category there was a reduction in the exemption levels between 1972 and 1978. Realized tariffs increased markedly, and in the case of the important machinery and electrical machinery categories, the increase was proportionately more than that of nominal tariffs.

An examination of total imports of capital goods over a longer period of time also reveals that there has been a tightening up on tariff reductions and exemptions in recent years. Table 2-3 shows that the average realized

Table 2-1

Nominal and Realized Tariff and Industrial-Product Tax Rates on Brazilian Imports, by Use of Product, 1977

Use of Product	*1977 Imports (CIF) (in U.S. $ million)*	*Percentage Share Of 1977 Imports*	*Tariff Rates (percent)*		*Industrial Product Tax (IPI) Rates (percent)*	
			Nominal[a]	*Realized*[b]	*Nominal*[a]	*Realized*[b]
Nondurable consumer goods	542.8	4.1	91.3	13.5	6.6	5.2
Durable consumer goods	157.2	1.2	115.0	24.7	24.1	8.6
Combustible fuels and lubricants	4,411.3	33.3	1.2	0.1	2.0	1.8
Intermediate products for agriculture	552.9	4.2	14.8	0.1	1.9	0.0
Intermediate products for industry	4,275.3	32.2	35.8	14.1	7.2	4.2
Construction materials	194.0	1.5	51.5	5.4	8.2	2.4
Capital goods for agriculture	71.3	0.5	29.6	8.6	5.3	0.7
Machines and tools	9.0		30.6	15.7	5.8	1.2
Other equipment	2.4		15.6	0.0	0.6	0.0
Transport equipment	59.9		30.0	7.9	5.4	0.7
Capital goods for industry	2,296.8	17.3	46.3	17.2	10.1	5.1
Office and scientific machinery	347.5		31.2	15.0	14.9	9.7
Tools	44.6		57.4	40.0	12.3	9.4
Machinery parts and accessories	284.4		46.9	20.4	7.9	4.6
Industrial machinery	1,218.7		41.1	11.7	7.3	2.7
Other fixed equipment	401.4		73.7	30.9	15.6	8.5
Transportation equipment[c]	755.5	5.7	49.0	5.4	7.8	1.1
Parts and accessories	394.7		67.9	9.1	9.0	1.5
Moving transport equipment	290.0		28.1	1.1	6.6	0.5
Fixed transport equipment	56.7		28.1	0.8	6.1	0.2
Miscellaneous	14.1		4.1	0.5	0.0	0.0
Total Capital-Goods Imports[d]	3,123.6	23.6	46.6	14.1	9.4	4.0
Total Imports	13,257.0	100.0	29.6	8.9	5.9	3.2

Source: Compiled from unpublished data kindly made available by CIEF.

[a]Nominal tax rates are those which would be in force if all taxes were paid.

[b]Realized tax rates were calculated as actual tax collections divided by CIF imports.

[c]Vehicles for personal use are included under durable consumer goods.

[d]Capital-goods imports include capital goods for agriculture, capital goods for industry, and transportation equipment.

Table 2-2
Nominal and Realized Tariff Rates on Brazilian Imports, by Import Classification, 1972 and 1978
(percent)

NBM Code	Product Group	Nominal[a] Tariff Rate 1972	Nominal[a] Tariff Rate 1978	Realized[b] Tariff Rate 1972	Realized[b] Tariff Rate 1978
84	Machinery	34.4	41.6	7.2	13.6
85	Electrical machinery	48.5	68.1	12.2	19.5
86	Railway equipment	28.5	34.9	0.3	0.7
87	Autos, trucks and tractors	39.9	79.4	10.4	12.6
88	Aircraft	7.0	39.5	0.9	0.2
89	Shipbuilding	7.8	7.0	0.08	0.1

Source: Ministério da Fazenda, *Comércio Exterior do Brasil: Importação, 1978* and unpublished data kindly made available by CIEF.

[a]Nominal tariff rates are those which would be in force if all tariffs were paid.

[b]Realized tariff rates were calculated as actual tariff collections divided by CIF imports.

tariff rate for all capital goods increase from an annual average of 9.6 percent for 1970-1972 to 13.5 percent in 1978. It is also interesting to note that the increase in realized tariffs for capital goods in 1976 and 1977 was preceded by a decline in 1973 and 1974. This decline was due to a liberalization in official industrial project approvals incorporating tariff exemptions and reductions, as exercised by the government in the euphoric high-growth years of 1972 and 1973.

Table 2-3
Realized Tariff Rates for Total Imports and Capital-Goods Imports, Selected Years, 1964-1978
(percent)

Year	All Imports	Capital-Goods Imports
1964	10.0	9.6
1967	10.8	10.3
1970	10.6	10.1
1971	9.7	9.3
1972	9.9	9.5
1973	8.7	8.3
1974	7.2	6.9
1976	10.0	16.2
1977	8.9	14.1
1978	8.1	13.5

Sources: Data for 1964-1974 were taken from Flávio Pinheiro de Castelo Branco, *Importações de Bens de Capital e Substituição de Importações,* Master's thesis, University of Brasília, 1976, p. 61. Data for 1976 to 1978 are from CIEF.

The structure of nominal, as well as realized, tariffs on capital goods can be seen in tables 2-1 and 2-4. Both tables present a consistent picture, although the level of disaggregation is greater in table 2-4. The latter presents, among other things, the 1976 tariff data as compiled and grouped in the format of the IBGE input-output table. Information is provided for sixteen capital-goods industries. Of these industries, industrial equipment and machinery is by far the most important. In 1976 products in this category accounted for one-third of Brazil's total capital-goods imports.[6] For this industry nominal tariffs averaged 40 percent. While a number of other capital goods industries are seen to exhibit similar tariff levels, tariff rates are markedly higher for the electrical equipment and electrical machinery industries, averaging 76 and 81 percent, respectively. The highest tariffs are present in the two industry categories where there are some durable consumer goods necessarily included. With both electronic equipment and motors and vehicle parts it is impossible to separate out final-use consumer items, for which tariffs tend to be higher. Since, unlike 1974-1975, the 1976-1979 period has witnessed little in the way of tariff changes, the 1976 nominal tariffs can be considered as reasonably representative of 1978-1979 tariff protection conditions.

In addition to tariffs, border taxes are also charged on imports. The industrial product tax (the IPI), formally a value-of-product tax, is levied on the CIF value of imports plus the nominal tariff. While it varies over products, for all capital goods the IPI averages around 10 percent. Tables 2-1 and 2-4 present a disaggregation of both nominal and realized IPI rates. Relatively low nominal rates exist for tractors (5 percent), agricultural equipment and machinery (6 percent), and industrial equipment and machinery (8 percent), while the highest rates prevail for electronic equipment (23 percent) and office and domestic equipment and machinery (19 percent). While the IPI rates are important in affecting net protection, the size of the IPI rates is determined by criteria evidently unrelated to commercial or industrialization policies. Imports must pay the state value added tax (ICM), in addition to the IPI. The ICM is currently a uniform 15 percent over all products for most states and is levied on top of the total value of the imported item at the CIF import price plus both the nominal tariff and IPI. Port taxes are also assessed, amounting to about 6 percent of the FOB value of imports. Unlike the tariff, the IPI, and the ICM, port taxes are never exempted. All of the border taxes—the IPI, the ICM, and port taxes—while affecting relative prices, are levied for objectives outside of commercial policy. Unlike the tariffs, these taxes have witnessed no appreciable changes during the 1973-1979 period.

While nominal tariffs have been increased since 1973, most of the increase in import restrictions observed since then has taken the form of expanding nontariff barriers. In 1975 an import deposit system was estab-

Table 2-4
Tariff and Fiscal Subsidy Rates for Capital Goods
(percent)

IBGE Sector Classification Code	*Industry*	*(1) Nominal Tariff Rate[a] 1976*	*(2) Realized Tariff Rate[b] 1976*	*(3) Nominal IPI Tax[a] Rate t_{IPI}*	*(4) Fiscal Subsidy via IPI and ICM Tax Credits[c] s_{IPI}*
121	Pumps and motors	45.5	13.0	6.0	22.4
122	Machine parts	49.4	28.3	14.5	20.8
123	Industrial equipment and machinery	40.2	9.2	7.6	21.0
124	Agricultural equipment and machinery	27.9	11.7	5.7	16.8
125	Office and domestic equipment and machinery	41.2	17.1	19.1	24.9
126	Tractors	26.7	4.9	5.2	23.0
131	Equipment for electric energy	55.4	17.1	7.0	19.4
132	Electric conductors	42.4	20.5	13.9	20.0
133	Electrical equipment	76.4	34.4	14.8	20.2
134	Electrical machinery	81.4	28.1	14.1	25.7
135	Electronic equipment	100.8	18.8	22.9	20.0
136	Communications equipment	60.9	42.0	14.4	26.5
142	Trucks and buses	37.6	8.7	10.7	26.0
143	Motors and vehicles parts	105.6	26.5	13.2	25.8
144	Shipbuilding	7.3	0.1	9.7	23.5
145	Railway and aircraft equipment	42.6	2.1	7.4	15.5

Sources: Estimates for Columns 1-3 were made from CIEF data as published in Ministério da Fazenda, *Comércio Exterior do Brasil: Importação, 1976.* Column 4 is from estimates undertaken in Affonso Celso Pastore, José Augusto Arantes Savasini and Joal de Azambuja Rose, "Quantificação dos Incentivos às Exportações," Fundação Centro de Estudos do Comércio Exterior, Rio de Janeiro, 1977.

[a]Nominal tax rates are those which would be in force if all taxes were paid. Their rates are weighted by imports.

[b]The realized tariffs were calculated as actual tariff collections divided by CIF imports.

[c]The fiscal subsidies via the IPI and ICM tax credits are estimates which were made with 1975 data.

lished and was continued in force until scrapped in the Economic Policy Reform Package of December 1979. During its existence this system involved a prior, 100 percent deposit of the FOB value of the imports for a one-year period with neither interest payments nor monetary correction. Unless exempted, the import deposit was applied to all capital-goods imports plus a wide range of other imports. With inflation running at some 40 percent annually during 1977-1978, the import deposit system implied an import surcharge of an amount more than 40 percent, depending upon the rate of interest foregone. Nominal effective interest rates averaged around 50 percent annually in 1977-1978 throughout the commercial banking system. Accepting this figure as the opportunity cost of money, the compulsory import deposit amounted to the equivalent of a 50 percent tariff levied on the FOB import price. The compulsory advance deposit for imports formally applied equally to most manufactured products. In practice, however, capital-goods imports were more likely to be made exempt from the deposit requirement than other included imports.

Beyond the indirect import restrictions, operating in one way or another through the market, direct controls over imports are also exercised and are most evident in the public sector. Government purchases have constituted a powerful force for the expansion of the Brazilian capital-goods sector.[7] Consequently, changes in government purchasing policy greatly affect the sector. The public sector, including government enterprises, has accounted for over 50 percent of total capital formation in Brazil in recent years.[8] In 1975 it was responsible for a large share of total imported capital goods, as a result of previously authorized and on-going investment programs.

Attempts to stem the tide of public-enterprise imports, for both balance-of-payments objectives and reasons of promoting the domestic capital-goods sector, have resulted in a series of measures. The public sector, along with government enterprises, is now prohibited from directly importing any consumer goods. Moreover, it is prohibited from importing or purchasing machinery, equipment, and vehicles produced abroad unless there is no satisfactory domestic equivalent available. In other words, the law of the national similar applies to all government purchases. In international bidding a 15 percent preference is given to domestic suppliers. Finally, a strict import budgeting on the part of public agencies and government enterprises has become standard practice. Each government organization must now submit, for approval by the president through the Planning Secretariat, an annual foreign-exchange budget, including a detailed justification for imports. The scrutiny of these budgets, in great part motivated by balance-of-payments considerations along with the desire of the Planning Secretariat to extend its own influence and power, has become increasingly meticulous and intense. The import budgeting requirement, and the approval for public imports, amounts to the imposition of a tacit import quota system. As a result of these efforts to budget and restrict government imports, a decline in such imports has been registered, much of which has been in the way of capital goods. A Planning Secretariat study of sixty-nine major state enterprises has shown that imports of these enterprises fell from about U.S. $3 billion in 1975 to U.S. $1.8 billion in 1977.[9]

The most complex part of the system of protection afforded to the Brazilian capital-goods industry has involved the system of incentives for industrial projects approved by government agencies, most notably the CDI (Conselho de Desenvolvimento Industrial). If a project obtains official approval, a series of incentives and benefits can be granted. While these incentives vary from program to program, they include: (1) the reduction of import duties, (2) the reduction of the border taxes due on imports, (3) the waiver of the prior deposit on imports, (4) access to official, subsidized credits, (5) exemption of IPI and ICM taxes for the purchase of domestically produced capital goods, (6) the granting of a fiscal subsidy (based upon a credit under the administration of the IPI tax) for purchasing domestically produced capital goods, and (7) the allowance of accelerated depreciation for income tax purposes for the case of domestic capital equipment. Since these benefits are substantial, most industrial investment projects are submitted for approval to the CDI, or to other agencies empowered to grant incentives. In the last five years the examination of investment projects has become much more thorough, and the reluctance to grant widespread tariff reductions on imported capital goods has grown. Concerted efforts have been made by government officials to reduce the import content of investment projects in the approval process.

The tightening up of the requirements for CDI approval is shown in table 2-5. In the early 1970s there was a rapid growth of approvals. In the period after its establishment in 1964 the CDI followed a policy of virtual indiscriminate granting of incentives. With the worsening balance-of-payments conditions beginning in 1974 the CDI became more selective. There was a sharp decline in the number of projects approved from a peak of 2,851 in 1973 to 130 in 1979. Accompanying this reduction, however, was an increase in the average size of project as a result of deliberate efforts of the CDI to discourage small projects. The average size of CDI-approved projects grew from the equivalent of U.S. $1.3 million in 1973 to U.S. $13.2 million in 1979.

Approval of investment projects by the CDI is based on a number of criteria.[10] Only if a project falls within certain broadly defined sectors can it obtain the official incentives provided by the CDI. The current priority sectors are: (1) capital goods, (2) basic metals and intermediate metal products, (3) chemicals, petrochemicals, and pharmaceutical products, (4) nonmetallic intermediate products, (5) automotive products, and (6) consumer goods. Since such a list omits very few industries, it is difficult

Table 2-5
CDI Approvals, 1971-1979

Year	*Number of Projects Approved*	*Total Value of Fixed Investment (U.S. $million)*
1971	755	n.a.
1972	1,904	n.a.
1973	2,851	3,592
1974	1,976	4,292
1975	871	2,028
1976	284	8,503
1977	203	4,213
1978	199	3,187
1979	130	1,716

Source: CDI, annual reports for various years.

Note: Cruzeiro values converted to U.S. dollars at the average official exchange rate for the year.

to discern what the "priorities" mean. Being a "priority" industry simply means that it is eligible, along with other "priority" industries, for the CDI incentives. Actually receiving the incentives may be another matter.

Within the comprehensive list of priority, or eligible, sectors certain industries have received more emphasis than others. Table 2-6 summarizes the approvals granted by CDI in 1977. As witnessed, consumer-goods industries have received a low priority, especially when considered in terms of their proportional importance in manufacturing output. The capital-goods sector is twice benefited. First, it is a priority sector itself, accounting for 15 percent of total fixed investment approval in CDI projects in 1977. Second, incentives granted to other sectors result in the purchase of the subsidized domestically produced capital goods. Imported machinery and equipment accounted for only 25.5 percent of the total approved purchases of such machinery and equipment in 1977, a percentage which is down substantially from previous years.

Although the CDI is the agency most frequently involved with official project approval and the concomitant approval for the granting of fiscal and financial incentives, other government agencies have similar functions. The BEFIEX program, also administered by the Ministry of Industry and Commerce, permits the granting of similar incentives, especially regarding the reduction of import taxes, for the commitment of a firm to export a certain amount as a part of its project. By 1977 total fixed investments undertaken as a part of BEFIEX projects amounted to U.S. $3.5 billion, of which over U.S. $3 billion was concentrated in the automotive sector. Yet, BEFIEX's role in other industries seems to be growing. It can grant larger import tax reductions than CDI (90 percent versus 80 percent), and BEFIEX has been acquiring a reputation as being more liberal in granting import permissions. Consequently, some investing firms are looking towards BEFIEX approval as an alternative to running the gauntlet with CDI on new projects. This has been notably the case with textile producers, which receive a very low priority with CDI. In addition to CDI and BEFIEX, still other government agencies are empowered to grant industrial incentives for projects. They include, most prominently, regional development institutions (SUDENE, SUDAM, SUFRAMA, GERES) and sectoral development agencies (SUDEPE, IBDF, EMBRATUR, EMBRAER, MOBRAL). The multitude of incentive granting agencies, all operating with different, and even conflicting, objectives, makes the coordination of industrial policy virtually impossible.

A further complication in admitting and coordinating the policies of incentives for industrial development relates to the import component of investment projects. While the CDI examines and approves the import content of its projects, subsequent analysis also occurs. After a project is approved by the CDI, or another approving agency, the import content of the project is further scrutinized by CACEX (the foreign trade department of the Banco do Brasil). According to the Law of the National Similar, a project cannot receive the benefits of the incentives system unless the imports carried out under the project have no comparable domestically produced counterpart. The examination for the "national similar" is the responsibility of CACEX. This examination, providing considerable authority to CACEX, takes place on several levels regarding both the technical characteristics of the equipment in question and price considerations. If the domestically produced good is technically comparable to the prospective import, the investor can still import the product if he can demonstrate that there would be uncommonly long delays in obtaining the domestic product, or if the domestic product is excessively expensive. The initiative for such an appeal, however, rests entirely with the investor.

What constitutes "excessively expensive" in the eyes of the policymakers, in this case CACEX officials, is obviously crucial in any evaluation of protection. Here the nominal tariff rate for the product in question (generally capital goods) plays an important role. The general rule applied by CACEX is that if the price of the imported equipment plus the tariff is lower than the price of the domestic counterpart, importation is allowed with the full enjoyment of the permissible incentives, for example, tariff reduction. Thus, it is the tariff that can decide whether a product can be imported or not.

The negotiating mechanism by which the examination of an industrial investment project's import content takes place is, in most cases, the formulation of a Participation Agreement (Acordo de Participação Nacional). Formalized tripartite discussions are held between the investor, CACEX officials, and the representatives of the relevant domestic capital

Table 2-6
Value of CDI Projects Approved in 1977

Sectors	Projects Approved	Project Amendments Approved	Machinery and Equipment Purchases Approved: Imported (CIF) (Cr$ millions)	Machinery and Equipment Purchases Approved: Domestically Produced (Cr$ millions)	Imported as a percent of total	Total Fixed Investment Approved (Cr$ millions)	Sectoral Share of Total Fixed Investment Approved Percent: 1977	Sectoral Share of Total Fixed Investment Approved Percent: 1976
I Capital-goods industries	62	146	1,772	1,864	48.7	7,350	15.1	2.0
II Basic metals and intermediate metal products	50	255	1,871	6,788	21.6	12,680	25.9	78.8
III Chemicals, petrochemicals, and pharmaceutical products	19	87	2,284	4,532	33.5	12,590	25.8	15.0
IV Nonmetallic intermediate products, cement, paper, and cellular products	18	70	947	7,069	11.8	10,744	22.0	2.1
V Automotive products	22	39	661	1,098	37.6	2,619	5.4	0.8
VI Consumer-goods industries	32	126	274	1,506	15.4	2,841	5.8	1.3
Totals	203	723	7,809	22,856	25.5	48,825	100.0	100.0

Source: Conselho de Desenvolvimento Industrial, *Relatório de Activadades, 1977*, pp. 10-80.

goods producers' associations (for example, ABDIB, ABIMAQ, or ABINEE). The purpose of these discussions is to examine the import content and the existence of suitable domestically produced counterparts. Once a Participation Agreement is reached concerning a project, the investor is permitted to import all the products agreed upon without further CACEX examination, even though the project may have a duration of several years.

The role of CACEX in the examination of the "national similar" and the formulation of Participation Agreements is critical. Essentially, CACEX grants import licenses, and in doing so it administers what amounts to a quota system on capital-goods imports. In the last four years CACEX has been under considerable pressure to reduce the imports of foreign equipment and machinery, both to strengthen Brazil's balance-of-payments situation and to provide greater protection for the domestic capital-goods industry. Much concern has been expressed in Brazil as to the magnitude of the so-called nationalization index, or simply the proportional domestic share of equipment purchases, for investment projects. Through its control over import licenses and the formulation of Participation Agreements, CACEX has sought to increase the nationalization index for capital goods purchases. What has happened is suggested in table 2-7.[11] The share of domestic capital-goods purchases under approved investment projects with Participation Agreements grew from 53 percent in 1973 to 82 percent in 1979.

Since 1975 the CACEX examination of the "national similar" has become more painstaking and exacting. The investor who wants to import machinery and equipment as part of an officially approved investment project is frequently put on the defensive. His list of proposed imports is scrutinized with care and even suspicion. CACEX officials and representatives of the capital-goods producers' associations attempt to reduce the import list by suggesting domestically produced counterparts. As stated, to

Table 2-7
CACEX Participation Agreements, 1973-1979

Year	Number of Agreements and Revisions	Total Capital-Goods Amount Negotiated (U.S. $ million)	Percentage Share of Capital-Goods: To be Purchased Domestically	Percentage Share of Capital-Goods: To be Imported
1973	145	689	52.7	47.3
1974	220	2,149	58.4	41.6
1975	264	2,714	62.4	37.6
1976	202	2,728	68.1	31.9
1977	192	2,838	76.6	23.4
1978	169	2,662	74.5	25.5
1979	180	1,763	82.4	17.6

Source: CACEX.

be able to import a piece of equipment with an existing national similar under an incentives program the investor must be able to demonstrate that the foreign-produced item is cheaper by more than the amount of the tariff. The level of the tariff is important, but equally so is the perseverance of the investor.

As noted, once imports under an incentive program are approved by CACEX, they may enter the country with tariff reductions. At the same time, the compulsory advance deposit on imports is also normally waived. In most cases foreign financing, generally accompanying capital-goods imports, results in the automatic exemption of the imports from the import deposit. While until several years ago full tariff exemptions were common, now the CDI is empowered to reduce tariffs for capital-goods imports only by either 50 or 80 percent.[12] The permissible reductions in the IPI and ICM taxes on imports are identical. Only in the special case of presidential approval can a 100 percent reduction, or full exemption, of import taxes be granted. Although the intent has been to eliminate the complete exemptions, there still have been several cases allowed.[13] While greatly reduced, the tariff reductions are still important and in fact are the general rule for the importation of capital goods. It has been estimated that about 80 percent of all capital-goods imports come into Brazil under some sort of incentives program. This is clearly reflected in the comparison of the theoretical nominal tariffs with the tariffs actually collected. The realized rates are substantially lower than the theoretical nominal rates. As was demonstrated in table 2-1, for all capital-goods imports in 1977 the realized tariff rate (that is, tariff collections divided by imports) was 14.1 percent, as compared to the theoretical nominal tariff of 46.6 percent. What this attests to in practice is not that the tariff levels for capital goods are low per se, but rather the way in which other mechanisms of import restrictions are employed. Tariffs nevertheless continue to exercise a role in these other mechanisms.

Fiscal Incentives

The reduction of taxes on imported machinery and equipment is an important form of fiscal inducement to spur industrial growth. With an overvalued exchange rate, reductions or exemptions for import taxes, and waivers for import deposits, the domestic purchaser price of imported capital goods appears relatively cheap. This has been the Brazilian historical experience. One effect of this policy of artificially reducing relative prices of imported capital goods in the last twenty-five years has been to foster a capital-intensive pattern of industrial development. In effect, the importation of capital equipment has been subsidized through exchange-rate overvaluation. Consequently, technology choice and changes in industrial structure have been effected.

Keeping the relative prices for imported capital goods low, as a conscious objective of industrial policy, also implies that the actual and potential profitability for the domestic capital-goods industry is kept low. In fact, a system of exchange-rate overvaluation and tariff exemptions for imported machinery and equipment discriminates against the domestic capital goods industry. However, it was in just such a general environment that the Brazilian capital-goods sector developed in the postwar period until the mid-1970s.[14] Despite the effects of discriminatory commercial policy, growth of the sector was impressive.

This situation, however, was soon to change. By the late 1960s and early 1970s there was a growing awareness of this discriminatory treatment on the part of the increasingly vocal and politically influential Brazilian capital-goods producers. There were growing pressures to redress this situation and undertake an active program of import substitution for capital goods. The permitted accelerated depreciation of domestically produced capital goods was an early attempt, dating back to September 1964, to compensate for discrimination against the domestic capital-goods industry.[15] The permissible depreciation rate for domestically produced capital goods was set at three times the normal rate for income tax purposes. In addition, a special agency (FINAME) of the National Development Bank was established to finance the purchase of domestically produced capital goods. Yet, it was not until the worldwide petroleum crisis and subsequent Brazilian balance-of-payments problems (compounded by the swelling of capital-goods imports related to CDI approvals) in the mid-1970s that further and more significant actions were undertaken. Decree Law 1335 of July 1974, implemented in March 1975, established a significant system of fiscal incentives for domestic producers of capital goods. These incentives go far in overcoming any discrimination stemming from an overvalued exchange rate and the apparent liberal granting of import tax reductions.

Decree Law 1335 stipulates that the purchase of domestically produced capital goods can be accompanied by the exemption of the IPI tax.[16] As a matter of course the ICM tax is exempted as well. The elimination of the IPI and ICM tax liabilities for domestic capital-goods purchases is necessary to put them on an even footing with imports if such border taxes have been exempted. Beyond the simple exemption of the IPI and ICM taxes, permitting a concomitant reduction in prices without changing unit profits, a direct fiscal subsidy is also allowable. The IPI tax, while technically a value-of-product tax, is in effect a value added tax as it is administered. Fiscal credits accumulate for a producing firm when it purchases intermediate inputs taxable by the IPI. These IPI fiscal credits can serve as the basis of a still greater reduction in tax liabilities for domestic capital-goods producers. This reduction constitutes a direct fiscal subsidy. It is identical to the direct fiscal subsidy that the firm would receive if the final capital-goods product were exported instead of sold domestically. In fact, Decree Law 1335 simply extends the fiscal incentives for manufactured exports, based upon the indirect tax system, to the internal sale of domestically produced capital goods.

The quantitative importance of the Decree Law 1335 fiscal subsidy for domestic capital-goods production varies over products because the IPI rates themselves vary, as does the degree of vertical integration in capital goods production. Column 4 of table 2-4 presents estimates from a study by Pastore et al. of the Decree Law 1335 fiscal subsidy element for sixteen capital goods industries.[17] As seen, while varying from 16 to 27 percent, the average fiscal subsidy averages about 20 percent of the *ex factory* price. The effect of the fiscal subsidies is to improve the competitiveness of domestically produced capital goods vis-à-vis imported capital goods. This is tantamount to a downward shift in the domestic supply curve for capital goods. The result, *ceteris paribus*, is an increase in domestic capital-goods production.

The granting of the fiscal subsidies under Decree Law 1335, like so many other aspects of Brazilian industrial policy, is discretionary. The Ministry of Finance administers the Decree Law 1335 regulations, and, although in practice it generally agrees with recommendations made by the CDI, final authority for granting the Decree Law 1335 fiscal incentives always rests with Finance. Unlike the CDI, which grants incentives primarily on the basis of industries to be promoted, the Decree Law 1335 subsidies by the Ministry of Finance focus on specific capital goods. Generally, the criteria relate to degree of sophistication and the period of time that domestic production has been taking place. If a product is not considered sufficiently "sophisticated," or it has been produced in Brazil for a long time, it will not receive the protection afforded by the Decree Law 1335 incentives. In 1977 the Ministry of Finance approved approximately 200 projects, corresponding roughly to the CDI projects approved during the same year. As such, there was a maximum of about U.S. $2.3 billion of domestic capital goods to which Decree Law 1335 incentives could possibly be applied. Nevertheless, these incentives were accompanied by high fiscal costs, raising questions among revenue-conscious policymakers. For 1978 SEPLAN estimates have put the fiscal cost of the Decree Law 1335 incentives at Cr $6 billion (that is, approximately U.S. $200 million).

In January 1979 the government announced that the fiscal credit subsidies for manufactured exports would be phased out over a five-year period and compensated for by real exchange-rate depreciation of comparable amount over the same period. Similarly, because of their same fiscal credit base under the prevailing legislation, the Decree Law 1335 fiscal credits were also to be phased out. The December 1979 economic policy reform package implemented these anticipated changes instantly, rather than over the previously announced five-year period. Accordingly, the December 1979 reforms technically eliminated the Decree Law 1335 fiscal credit for domestic capital-goods purchases. The IPI exemptions (also covered under Decree Law 1335), however, still exist and are still administered in the same discretionary fashion.

Financial Incentives

In addition to the fiscal incentives allowed to the Brazilian capital-goods sector, financial incentives are also provided as a part of official policy to promote the industry. These take the form of interest rate subsidies through various official financing programs. By far the most important official financial support for the capital-goods industry comes from the BNDE (National Development Bank) system. Under the BNDE system an important source has been the Special Agency for Industrial Financing (FINAME). Established in 1964, FINAME possesses a "special program" for the financing of sales of domestically produced capital goods. Now accounting for about two-thirds of total FINAME commitments, the special program commitments for capital-goods sales in 1977 totaled Cr $19.7 billion (about U.S. $1.4 billion at the prevailing exchange rates).[18]

The regulations governing the special program in 1978 permitted FINAME financing for domestic capital-goods sales at rates of interest in nominal terms of up to 8 percent annually plus full monetary correction. The average nominal rate of interest on all FINAME loans in 1978 was 4.7 percent, while the monetary correction for the year was 40.6 percent. Thus, for 1978 the average nominal effective interest rate charged for FINAME financing of capital-goods suppliers credits was 45.3 percent, as compared to the prevailing commercial banking rates of the order of 50-55 percent. To the extent that the official monetary correction charged is less than the rate of inflation, the subsidization of FINAME credit is apparent.[19]

The effect of the FINAME special program credits, extended at subsidized interest rates, is to enhance the competitiveness of the Brazilian capital goods producer in the domestic market. Purchasing a domestically produced capital good with FINAME special program credits can serve to offset a price advantage that an imported equivalent may possess. The price effect of these subsidized credits can be expressed on a value-of-product basis through an examination of the present value of loan repayments. The credit subsidy effect is thus estimated as

$$\frac{P}{P} = \frac{P - P'}{\mathrm{P}} = 1 - \frac{\mathrm{i}'}{i}\left[\frac{1 - \dfrac{1}{(1+i)^n}}{1 - \dfrac{1}{(1-i')^n}}\right] \tag{2.1}$$

where

P = price of capital good
P' = present value of payments at subsidized interest rate, discounted at market rate
i' = nominal effective interest rate charged on loan (subsidized rate)
i = market interest rate
n = loan term, years

If $i' = 45.3$ percent annually, $i = 50$ percent annually, and $n = 10$ years, the subsidy is equal to 8.8 percent. Thus, for 1978 it was estimated that these subsidies permitted an 8.8 percent reduction in price to the purchase, in relation to the firm's *ex factory* price. In 1977 the monetary correction index, with which all FINAME loans are now adjusted, lagged considerably behind the rate of inflation. Consequently, the financial subsidies provided to the capital-goods industries were greater than they were in 1978. The 1977 credit subsidies were estimated to have amounted to 29.4 percent on a value-of-product basis. With the acceleration of the inflation in 1979 the magnitude of the subsidies increased again, resulting in substantial credit subsidies in 1980 emanating from the quickened inflation rates and the pre-fixing of monetary correction.

The subsidized credits provided through FINAME for the sale of domestically produced capital goods in the internal market are only one form of credit subsidy provided to the Brazilian capital-goods industries. Another form, which we have not succeeded in quantifying, is the subsidized credit provided to the capital-goods producers themselves for the installation or expansion of productive capacity. As evidenced by the First National Development Plan for 1975-1978, the capital-goods sector was declared a priority area. As a result, considerable BNDE lending activity for capacity expansion was concentrated in this sector. Since much of this lending activity has involved long-term loans and terms with pre-fixed monetary correction set at a maximum of 20 percent per annum, negative real interest rates on such lending have been commonplace. The total magnitude of these credit subsidies has been considerable, although most probably not as large as the FINAME subsidies.[20]

In addition to credits provided for domestic market sales and for capital goods production facilities, export financing for capital goods is also available both for export production and export sales. Dating back to 1971, the Brazilian Central Bank has provided a mechanism designed to channel working capital through the commercial banking system to export-producing firms. Credit is provided for up to a year and eligibility is based upon export performance. The interest rates, originally fixed at 8 percent annually without monetary correction, varied between 8 and 12 percent during the 1978-1979 period. As such, the credit subsidies can be considerable. While not restricted to capital-goods exports, these credit subsidies for such exports in 1975 ranged up to 14 percent of industry exported value (appendix table B-3).

Long-term financing for manufactured export sales is provided by CACEX and has been primarily for capital goods. In 1977 these operations, funded through a facility called FINEX, amounted to about one-fourth of the estimated total value of capital-goods exports. CACEX will finance up to 85 percent of the FOB value of exports in dollars at an interest rate of between 7 and 8.5 percent annually. These rates of interest are slightly less than those prevailing for official suppliers' credits from most countries. The permitted maturities range from 5 years to 8-10 years depending upon the size and type of transaction, with large capital-goods export orders receiving the most privileged terms.

Protection of Intermediate Inputs

A regime of overvalued exchange rates must necessarily be accompanied by other forms of import restrictions. These restrictions on imports are also used for protecting certain industries. In Brazil, as in other countries where import restrictions have been employed to spur import-substituting industrialization, nearly all industrial activities are affected by higher costs brought about by protection in industries supplying intermediate and capital goods inputs. The Brazilian capital-goods sector is no exception. Protection afforded to Brazilian steel producers of intermediate inputs has adversely affected the competitiveness of the capital-goods sector. As the effective protection literature vividly points out, the effects of protection on inputs must be considered in any assessment of net protection.[21]

A recent study of effective protection in Brazil conducted by Neuhaus and Lobato has employed realized tariffs to approximate protection.[22] Their estimates, using 1975 tariff information and the 1970 IBGE input-output table, included separate calculations for the protection on inputs. They are presented in column (1) of table 2-8. We have used these (Corden method) Neuhaus and Lobato estimates to calculate the proportional effect on *ex factory* prices that protection on inputs can exercise for sixteen capital-goods industries.[23] These estimates are presented as column (2) in table 2-8. They range from a low of 2.4 percent (shipbuilding) to 10.8 percent (trucks and buses). For industrial equipment and machinery, the estimate of the price increase due to protection on inputs is a very low 3.4 percent.

It should be noted that we believe the effect of protection on inputs to be underestimated. This is because we feel that the use of realized tariffs substantially understates the difference between domestic and international prices. A vivid and important example of this difficulty is the case of steel imports. Steel products constitute one of the most important intermediate inputs for capital-goods production, accounting for 8.13 percent of the value of final product in the different capital-goods industries.[24] The 1975 realized tariff rate for steel imports was only 1 percent. Yet, the imports of steel are simply not restricted through tariff measures. The government steel council CONSIDER establishes and administers a quota for steel imports. Consequently, the 1 percent realized tariff rate understates domestic and international price differences. In fact, some Brazilian capital-goods producers have complained that the domestic prices of some internally produced specialty steels (for example, stainless) are over twice the current international prices.[25]

The underestimation of the effects from protection on inputs results in an overestimate of protection afforded to the production processes in question. If, on the other hand, all inputs could be freely imported at world prices, the estimates of net protection would be larger. In the absence of trade restrictions, the input content of Brazilian capital-goods production would be higher. The low import content for most capital-goods industries is indicated in column (3) of table 2-8. For the industrial equipment and machinery industry total imports used in production by the industry accounted for less than 2 percent of the industry's output in 1970.

Net Protection

After having discussed some of the individual policies relating to relative prices for the Brazilian capital-goods industry, we are ready to consider them together and in doing so return to the central question considered in this chapter: To what extent is the Brazilian capital-goods sector protected or unprotected by the constellation of economic policies affecting it? Appendix 2B presents a measurement technique for examining net protection. The measure of net protection for product j, (p_j) incorporates the effects of import restrictions, fiscal incentives, financial subsidies, the protection on inputs, and exchange-rate overvaluation. The rationale is to compare the possible prices to buyers for imports and domestically produced products after the effect of economic policies is taken into account. To undertake this comparison possible prices are expressed in relation to unit import CIF prices and unit domestic *ex factory* prices. This means that prior to any adjustments for economic policies the ratio of the duty-free import CIF price and the *ex factory* domestic product price is 1.00. After adjustments for import restrictions, fiscal incentives, and financial subsidies, adjustments are

Table 2-8
Information on the Effects of Economic Policies on Imported and Domestically Produced Capital Goods

IBGE Sector Classification Code	Industry	(1) Realized Tariff Protection on Inputs[a] (Corden Method) (percent)	(2) Estimated Domestic Product Price Increase due to Protection Inputs (percent)	(3) Import Content in Final Product[b] (percent)	(4) Import Price to Buyer without Tax Reductions, ($\alpha = {}^{P}M0$)	(5) Domestically Produced Product Price to Buyers[c]: w/o D.L.1335 Incentive and without Financial Subsidies ($\gamma = {}^{P}D0$)	(6) Domestically Produced Product Price to Buyers[c]: with D.L.1335 Incentives and Financial Subsidies ($\gamma = {}^{P}D1$)	(7) Coefficient of Distortion (θ)
121	Pumps and motors	16.22	8.6	6.2	2.260	1.169	0.638	1.386
122	Machine parts	10.53	4.3	3.8	2.454	1.317	0.654	1.343
123	Industrial equipment and machinery	11.24	3.4	1.9	2.222	1.237	0.644	1.340
124	Agricultural equipment and machinery	11.59	5.1	2.1	2.042	1.166	0.694	1.351
125	Office and domestic equipment and machinery	14.88	7.5	7.5	2.421	1.320	0.613	1.375
126	Tractors	14.94	8.3	6.3	2.026	1.205	0.632	1.382
131	Equipment for electric energy	9.92	4.2	8.1	2.399	1.181	0.668	1.342
132	Electric conductors	6.67	4.0	25.2	2.352	1.260	0.662	1.340
133	Electric equipment	11.16	4.3	3.2	2.816	1.270	0.660	1.343
134	Electrical machinery	12.69	4.7	5.2	2.867	1.262	0.605	1.347
135	Electronic equipment	14.55	5.5	10.0	3.325	1.363	0.662	1.355
136	Communications equipment	15.09	7.1	5.1	2.604	1.267	0.597	1.371
142	Trucks and buses	17.43	10.8	1.6	2.239	1.223	0.602	1.408
143	Motors and vehicle parts	13.42	6.0	2.3	3.164	1.252	0.604	1.360
144	Shipbuilding	6.42	2.4	2.4	1.841	1.212	0.627	1.324
145	Railway and aircraft equipment	11.26	3.8	2.2	2.248	1.185	0.707	1.338

Sources: Columns 1 and 2 were based on estimates in Paulo Neuhaus and Helenamaria Lobato, "Protecáo Efectiva à Indústria no Brasil, 1973-1975," Fundaçáo Centro de Estudos do Comércio Exterior, Rio de Janeiro, 1978. Column 3 was obtained from IBGE, *Matriz de Relações Interindustrias: Brasil 1970* (Rio de Janeiro: IBGE, 1976). See text and appendix 2B for a discussion of the methods of computation for the remaining columns.

then made for other policies through a coefficient of distortion θ, reflecting the effects of (1) exchange rate overvaluation, and (2) protection on inputs.[26] Since there is a great deal of administrative discretion involved under different industrial policy schemes, a range of net protection is estimated.

Column (4) of table 2-8 presents the price ratio to the buyer of imported capital goods if all import taxes are charged. This would be the case if the product in question were to be imported outside an official investment project scheme, that is, without obtaining official approval. The Law of the National Similar is not applicable and full duties are charged.[27] The combined effect of the taxes and import deposit is roughly to double the CIF import price. On a unit CIF import price basis, the purchase price for an average product in the industrial equipment and machinery category is 2.22 times the unit price if all import charges are levied. For electrical equipment, where there is a higher tariff, the comparable figure is 2.82. In practice, some capital-goods users have preferred to import some capital goods in this manner, claiming that the uncertainty and delays of the official incentive schemes were sometimes too great to offset any potential private benefits to the investor.

If there are tariff and import tax reductions, the buyer's price of the imported product drops accordingly. In the case of industrial equipment and machinery the prices for a 50 percent and an 80 percent import tax reduction, as possibly granted by CDI, are 1.34 and 1.13, respectively. If there is a 100 percent reduction (although rare), the buyer's price for all capital-goods categories is 1.05.

The purchase price of the domestically produced product, beginning from an equal unitary *ex factory* price, depends upon whether the fiscal incentives and financial subsidies are granted. In their absence the buyer's price ratios for the domestic product for the sixteen capital-goods industries are given in column (5) of table 2-8. They range from 1.17 (pumps and motors) to 1.36 (electronic equipment), differing because of differences in the IPI over products.

Column (6) of table 2-8 lists the buyer's price if full allowable fiscal incentives and financial subsidies are granted. As demonstrated, these Decree Law 1335 incentives and official financing arrangements make a very important difference in the possible buyer's price. The permissible prices average around 0.65 of the original *ex factory* price, with that for industrial equipment and machinery being 0.64. As is demonstrated in table 2-8, the production subsidies, if fully applied, can result in substantial price reductions. These subsidies are indeed powerful policy instruments.

The coefficient of distortion θ, as noted above, consists of two components: (1) any departure in practice from a shadow exchange rate, and (2) the estimated domestic product price increase due to protection on inputs. Accordingly, θ reflects distortions in the prices facing producers and purchasers of capital goods. The use of θ adjusts for those distortions, which have resulted from economic policies not dealing specifically with the industry in question. A producer will make the comparison between the actual buyer price in the market for imports and domestically produced goods, but the choice for society as a whole should more appropriately reflect distortions in the exchange rate and in the prices of inputs due to protection of those inputs. Whether or not a production process is protected or disprotected in a social sense depends upon an entire constellation of economic policies. The use of the coefficient of distortion θ adjusts for the effects of two major policy instruments on the competitiveness of a certain industry.

Estimates of the coefficient of distortion θ are listed in column (7) of table 2-8. As seen, θ varies over industries (or products). This is because the estimated domestic product price increase due to protection on inputs [column (2)] varies from industry to industry. The coefficient of distortion also reflects exchange-rate overvaluation, which affects all industries uniformly. Based upon existing estimates of what would be an equilibrium exchange rate, we have arbitrarily chosen 30 percent as the degree of exchange-rate overvaluation.[28]

Different combinations of policies actually implemented of course imply different effects on net protection. Table 2-9 presents some alternatives under present administrative procedures. A net protection measure p_j greater than 1.00 indicates the industry is protected, while a p_j less than 1.00 denotes that the combined effect of economic policies serves to leave the industry negatively protected. A p_j of 1.00 would indicate neutrality of all commercial policy, favoring neither imports or domestic production.

Column (1) of table 2-9 presents the measure of net protection with full import charge levies and without concessionary fiscal and financial subsidies.[29] The p_j's range from a low 1.15 (Shipbuilding) to as much as 1.86 (motors and vehicle parts). In no case is any capital-goods industry disprotected. The net protection for the important industrial equipment and machinery industry, under these circumstances, amounts to 34 percent. These estimates indicate that if all the legal tariffs and charges were levied on imports, the subsidization of domestic production would not be required to protect the domestic capital-goods industry. It does illustrate, however, that the elimination of the compulsory import deposit, without domestic production subsidies or compensating devaluation, would leave many capital-goods industries unprotected.

The column (1) estimates of possible net protection have great relevance to actual protection. Many investment projects are not eligible for government investment incentives. Consequently, if capital-goods imports are to be undertaken, the prevailing tariffs and import deposit levels are applicable. Accordingly, the levels of protection afforded to the capital-goods industries appear to be high, although not outrageously so. However, to the

Table 2-9
Net Protection (p_j) under Alternative Program Schemes for Sixteen Capital-Goods-Producing Industries

IBGE Sector Classification Code	Industry	*Without Tariff and Border Tax Reduction via Official Programs: that is, Full Tariffs*		*With 100% Tariff and Border Tax Reduction via Official Programs ($\alpha = 1.0$)*	
		(1) Without Concessionary Incentives and Subsidies for Domestic Production ($\gamma = 0$)	*(2) With Full Concessionary Incentives and Subsidies for Domestic Production ($\gamma = 1$)*	*(3) Without Concessionary Incentives and Subsidies for Domestic Production ($\gamma = 0$)*	*(4) With Full Concessionary Incentives and Subsidies for Domestic Production ($\gamma = 1$)*
121	Pumps and motors	1.39	2.56	0.65	1.19
122	Machine parts	1.39	2.71	0.59	1.17
123	Industrial equipment and machinery	1.34	2.58	0.63	1.22
124	Agricultural equipment and machinery	1.30	2.18	0.67	1.13
125	Office and domestic equipment and machinery	1.33	2.87	0.58	1.25
126	Tractors	1.22	2.32	0.63	1.21
131	Equipment for electric energy	1.51	2.68	0.66	1.18
132	Electrical conductors	1.39	2.65	0.62	1.19
133	Electrical equipment	1.65	3.18	0.62	1.19
134	Electrical machinery	1.69	3.52	0.62	1.30
135	Electronic equipment	1.80	3.66	0.62	1.16
136	Communications equipment	1.50	3.18	0.61	1.29
142	Trucks and buses	1.30	2.64	0.61	1.25
143	Motors and vehicle parts	1.86	3.85	0.62	1.29
144	Shipbuilding	1.15	2.22	0.66	1.27
145	Railway and aircraft equipment	1.42	2.38	0.66	1.12

Source: Information in table 2-8. For method of computation see text and Appendix B.

extent that the effects of protection on intermediate inputs are understated, as we believe to be the case, our estimates of possible net protection in column (1) are biased upward.

Combining the existing tariffs and import charges with the full complement of subsidies on domestic production provides very high levels of net protection. This is demonstrated in column (2) of table 2-9. In every capital-goods industry net protection is at least 200 percent. Such protection is clearly excessive. However, in practice this is not the normal case. If full domestic subsidies were allowed, as a part of an official investment project, there would be a reduction of the import taxes actually charged. Thus the column (2) estimates, *ceteris paribus*, are a maximum and an extreme.

An opposite, and equally unlikely, extreme is the case of a 100 percent reduction of import taxes via official programs, without any allowable domestic production subsidies. These estimates are presented in column (3) of table 2-9. In this case all the domestic capital-goods industries are disprotected by policies. The estimates demonstrate that in the absence of tariff protection and domestic production subsidies, some protection of the capital-goods industries is necessary to overcome the disprotection afforded by exchange-rate policy and the protection of intermediate inputs. These latter two policies discriminate against the capital-goods sector, as well as against other manufacturing activities.

As is the case with all of the estimates presented in table 2-9, column (3) merely presents *possible* magnitudes of net protection under different policy applications and mixes. However, the column (3) estimates of net protection are unlikely to be those actually observed in practice, for two reasons. First, the 100 percent reduction in import taxes is an extreme, to be granted only under exceptional circumstances by presidential decree. The present reductions are of either 50 or 80 percent, depending upon the nature of the project, with the latter figure being the maximum allowable reduction under the CDI procedures. Consequently, the disprotection evidenced in column (3) of table 2-9 is overstated. Nevertheless, for even a 50 percent reduction in import taxes, again without domestic production subsidies, the net protection p_j for the Industrial Equipment and Machinery industry would be 0.81. In other words, in this situation, without domestic production subsidies and with the waiving of the prior import deposit, the domestic industry is still disprotected.

A second reason why the possible levels of protection (that is, disprotection) are unlikely in practice concerns the use of the domestic production subsidies. In a project submitted to the CDI, or another comparable agency, for the receipt of official government incentives, it is improbable for that project to be granted tariff reductions but no domestic production subsidies. The two types of incentive systems in practice go together, although in fact they may apply to different capital-goods components within a project.

Column (4) of table 2-9 presents the more likely case of both allowed tariff incentives (reductions) and domestic production subsidies for an investment project. As seen, even with the rare 100 percent reductions in import taxes, the existence and use of domestic production subsidies is sufficient to ensure positive net protection to every Brazilian capital-goods industry. Ranging from 12 to 30 percent for all capital-goods industries, the measure of net protection under these conditions for industrial equipment and machinery is 22 percent. Naturally, in the case of less than a 100 percent reduction in import taxes, that is, a 50 or 80 percent reduction, net protection is even higher.

Comparing column (1) and column (4) in table 2-9, it can be seen that the subsidies on domestic production are a more important form of protection for the Brazilian capital-goods industry than the tariffs. These subsidies can be substantial and can result in very high levels of protection.

In concluding that rather high levels of net protection for the Brazilian capital-goods sector exist, some important qualifications must be borne in mind, the effect of each being to reduce our estimates of net protection. First, the net effect of the financial subsidies may be overstated. Frequently, subsidized credit is furnished to purchasers of foreign capital goods. The effects of this subsidy, however, have not been incorporated into our measure, as outlined in appendix 2B. Second, as stated, we feel that the effect of protection on inputs has been understated. This serves to bias downward our estimate of the coefficient of distortion, resulting consequently in an overestimate of net protection.[30] Third, the full fiscal incentives are not granted to all types of capital goods. As a result our estimates incorporating the production subsidies can be thought of as measures of net *possible* protection. If provided, the fiscal subsidies can boost the protection to extremely high levels. Finally, some qualification is necessary since we are analyzing only the capital-goods sector. What matters in the overall system of incentives is the position of the sector relative to other sectors of the economy, and it is clear that many other manufacturing industries enjoy very high levels of protection.

Some nonquantifiable considerations are also important in the discussion of net protection provided to domestic producers in the home market. There are some competitive elements which cannot be captured in price comparisons. Servicing is especially important for capital goods, and the ready access to nearby servicing and parts presumably gives domestically produced capital goods something of a competitive advantage in relation to imports. On the other hand, technology transfer and technical training abroad for employees are cited as reasons why some capital-goods purchasers have a preference for imported capital goods. Some disgruntled domestic capital-goods producers also cite the capacity and willingness of major foreign capital-goods suppliers to provide large kickbacks for purchase orders, especially from public enterprises, as reasons for a preference for imports.

The high observed levels of net protection for the Brazilian capital-goods sector raise an important normative question. Should the capital-goods industries be protected? We are willing to concede, based upon previous Brazilian experience, that the arguments that there should be some protection are strong. Certainly, the sector should not suffer disprotection. Nevertheless, it appears that the observed levels of net protection, when full domestic production subsidies are applied, are excessive. The present policy appears to be one of protectionary overkill, applied discretionarily by well-meaning technocrats.

One of the major features of table 2-9 is the horizontal variation of net protection afforded to a single industry (or firm) under different, discretionary applications of existing policy and incentive schemes. These differences appear to be greater than the differences across the capital-goods industries within the context of a given policy application (any column in table 2-9). Obviously, getting all the incentives possible is extremely important for an individual firm in determining its profitability. It is no wonder then that firms place such an emphasis on their government relations. The government, or more accurately, individual government agencies, have the persisting power, through their ability to grant or deny incentive concessions, to make or break individual business enterprises. The profitability of an individual firm is as much dependent upon its governmental relations as it is upon its productive efficiency. Accordingly, firms find themselves obliged to operate in a political milieu and to respond to political considerations. It is in part for this reason that the capital-goods producing firms in Brazil are among the most politically articulate.

This discretionary nature of the system of protection for capital goods is its most pernicious element. As has been indicated, the magnitude of protection actually provided can vary widely. And in actual practice it does so on a case-by-case basis. There is little, if any, evenness or automaticity in the system. Individual purchasers of capital goods are affected by separate government decisions, perhaps in a variety of agencies, related to the granting or nongranting of a multitude of investment incentives. Domestic producers of capital goods are faced by a continual uncertainty, not knowing whether the fiscal production subsidies will be granted from one sale to the next.

As currently organized, the overall operation of the system, however well-intentioned the officials administering it, is bound to be capricious and uneven. Moreover, with all decisions made on a case-by-case basis, the system is potentially corruptable and highly dependent upon the common sense, fairness, and personal integrity of those government officials making decisions on the granting of the so-called investment incentives. The evidence as to the actual corruption of the system is spotty, not to mention controversial, but anecdotes abound.

To be sure, the evolution and operation of the system are best understood within the framework of bureaucratic politics. Different agencies and their officials seek to maximize their own institutional and personal authority. Withholding or granting privileges or investment incentives is both an expression and a result of power. The jockeying for power and policymaking authority has made the operation of the rules affecting the administration of protection for the Brazilian capital-goods industry highly discretionary. It is equally clear that to change this system is likewise a highly political act, affecting both the concerned industries and the pecking order of governmental agencies.

The discretionary nature of the protection system is an integral characteristic of Brazilian economic policy. A general attempt to reduce the level of discretionary policymaking regarding incentives, while highly desirable, is unlikely to be successful in the longer run. A cleaning up of the system, involving greater incentive automaticity and horizontal equity among firms, would merely pave the way for future discretionary actions. Pressures would build for exceptions, exemptions, special treatment, and other incentive favors. The centralization of authority to grant such favors becomes an important potential political and/or financial resource. An attempt to clean up the system and reduce its myriad of discretionary schemes was evident in the announced economic policy reforms of December 1979. However, shortly after the reforms, exceptions and other types of backsliding began to occur. By mid-1980 the system was not much different from that which existed in late 1979, prior to the sweeping December 1979 economic policy reforms.

A further question is raised by the use of subsidies for domestic capital-goods production. Like the policy of exchange-rate overvaluation combined with tariff exemptions, the effect of the use of subsidies for domestic capital-goods production is to lower the relative cost to the investor of using capital in production. Thus, a further cost of subsidizing the development of the Brazilian capital-goods industry may be to continue the capital-intensive industrial development in other sectors of the economy.

Indications of Competitiveness

In examining the effects of economic policies, our estimates of net protection have made the assumption that CIF import prices and domestic *ex factory* prices are the same. In reality, of course, they are not. There are other factors which affect economic costs. The extent to which domestic and international prices do compare reflects the competitiveness of Brazilian capital goods. It is clear that Brazilian commercial policies affect the competitiveness of Brazilian products. Given these policies, it is possible to make some price comparisons to examine the actual competitiveness of

Brazilian capital goods under present circumstances. Given that the development of the capital-goods sector is an objective of government policy, the question is whether, in view of present price competitiveness, Brazilian producers actually need the protection that government policy frequently provides.

Before making some actual price comparisons of Brazilian capital goods with their internationally produced counterparts, two general observations can be made, suggesting an improvement in Brazilian competitiveness and efficiency in producing capital goods. First, Brazilian exports of capital goods have grown steadily and dramatically. Between 1973 and 1976 capital-goods exports grew at an annual average rate of 49 percent, much more than did Brazilian exports in general, or even manufactured exports.[31] While these exports are still small relative to total domestic output, their growth suggests an increase in competitiveness. Moreover, the observed variety of Brazilian capital-goods exports, ranging from simple machinery to heavy armaments, suggests that reasonable competitiveness has been obtained along a broad front.

It is true that one of the reasons accounting for the increased international competitiveness and growth of Brazilian manufactured exports has been a package of export subsidies. All indirect taxes are rebated for manufactured exports, and there has also been a pure fiscal subsidy element, as presented in column (4) of table 2-4. In addition, there is a credit subsidy, provided principally through the provision of heavily subsidized working capital for the purpose of export production. The combined magnitude of the export subsidies can be substantial for capital goods, ranging from 20 percent (electronic equipment) of the exported product's value to 36.5 percent (tractors).[32] It should be noted, however, that (1) the export subsidies were established in the late sixties, and until December 1979 there was little appreciable change in their magnitude, especially for the fiscal subsidies; and (2) the subsidies for manufactured export were for most industries less than the amount of exchange-rate overvaluation. Consequently, while the export subsidies may be important in having promoted Brazil's exports of capital goods, they alone are an insufficient explanation.

Given the magnitude of the subsidies for the export of capital goods and the level of protection in the domestic market, it is possible to compare the two. The question is whether, given export promotional and import protectionist policies, profitability is greater in producing for the export market or the domestic market. For our comparison we have used the estimates of net import protection (p_j) assuming full domestic production subsidies and total tariff exemptions (column (4) of table 2-9). A measure of net export promotion can be constructed analogously using the estimates of the fiscal and credit subsidies for export. In the case of every capital-goods industry, net import protection exceeded net export promotion.[33] In other words, with the use of full domestic production subsidies, production for the domestic market is more profitable than production for export. The use of the full domestic production subsidies provides a net anti-export bias for the Brazilian capital-goods sector. This anti-export bias, however, while still existent, is not as large if only full tariffs are used to protect the domestic market.

A second general indication of improved competitiveness for the Brazilian capital-goods sector can be seen in the movement of relative prices within Brazil. Over the last ten years the prices of capital goods have declined relative to prices for other industrial products. Table 2-10 demonstrates this decline. While saying nothing about absolute international competitiveness, such a movement in relative prices internally suggests that Brazil's competitiveness has improved over time. The relative decline in capital-goods prices is most likely related to the significant technological progress occurring in the sector. For example, as a following discussion will show, it has been estimated that the annual proportional rate of Hicks neutral technological progress for four capital-goods producing industries ranged between 18 and 24 percent for the 1971-1975 period.[34]

Table 2-11 presents some price comparisons for Brazilian and foreign-produced capital goods. Prices are given in U.S. dollars FOB and are direct firm price quotations. For the Brazilian products the price effects of the incentives for manufactured exports are included. In other words, tax rebates

Table 2-10
Brazilian Wholesale Industrial Price Indexes, 1970-1980 (First Semester 1969 = 100)

Year	*(1) All Industrial Products*	*(2) Machinery*	*(3) Relative Prices of Machinery [(2)/(1)] × 100*	*(4) Electrical Machinery and Equipment*	*(5) Relative Prices of Electrical Machinery and Equipment [(4)/(1)] × 100*
1969 (first semester)	100	100	100	100	100
1970	121	114	94	117	97
1971	142	130	92	128	90
1972	165	151	92	143	87
1973	190	168	88	164	86
1974	246	203	83	200	81
1975	317	261	82	246	78
1976	432	356	82	336	78
1977	601	504	84	462	77
1978	813	688	85	629	77
1979	1,265	989	78	959	75
1980 (June)	2,434	1,643	68	1,809	74

Source: *Conjuntura Econômica*, various issues.

Table 2-11
Some Price Comparisons between Brazilian and Foreign-Produced Capital Goods

Industry and Product	*(1) Price Quotations of Brazilian Product (U.S. $ FOB)*	*(2) Price of Comparable Foreign Product (U.S. $ FOB)*	*(3) Country of Origin for Foreign Product*	*(4) Ratio of Brazilian Price to Foreign Price (1)/(2)*
Machine Tools				
Bench Lathe				
a.	850	820	Taiwan	1.03
b.	1,550	1,380	USA	1.12
Parallel Lathe				
a.	16,811	11,806	Czechoslovakia	1.42
b.	9,422	9,925	Argentina	.94
Bench Perforator				
a.	386	363	Rhodesia	1.06
b.	862	1,363	USA	.60
Textile Machinery				
Spinning Machine				
a.	40,968	40,000	Europe	1.02
b.	41,735	40,000	Europe	1.04
Looms				
a.	3,661	3,000	South Korea	1.22
b.	7,674	9,500	Europe	.81
Agricultural Machinery				
Automated Harvestor				
a.	29,411	23,000	Europe	1.27
b.	32,866	23,000	Europe	1.42
c.	29,330	23,000	Europe	1.27
d.	24,203	23,000	Europe	1.05
Tractors w/Wheels				
a.	7,083	8,900	Europe	.79
b.	9,608	10,404	USA	.92
c.	9,383	7,658	Europe	1.22

Source: EMBRAMEC, "Competitividade da Indústria Brasileira de Bens de Capital," unpublished paper, 1978.

and export subsidies are reflected in the Brazilian price quotations. Also, the Brazilian export prices are provided at the present, overvalued exchange rate. Out of the seventeen product price comparisons listed in table 2-10, in only three cases were Brazilian prices more than 30 percent greater than the price of the comparable foreign product. In most cases the prices were quite similar. If these products are at all representative, the indications are that reasonable degrees of international competitiveness have been attained under present policies.

Similar evidence is apparent in a BNDE study of road-building machinery and equipment. Again, direct FOB price comparisons in U.S.

dollars were made, based upon producer price quotations. In thirty separate price comparisons of comparable products, only eighteen were found to disfavor Brazil.[35] Of these, eight comparisons were concentrated for heavy-treaded tractors, where Brazilian prices seem to be substantially higher than international price levels. The remaining price comparisons demonstrated great similarity in Brazilian and international export prices. Brazil seems to have attained some degree of international competitiveness in road-building machinery and equipment with the exception of heavy-treaded tractors.

Concluding Remarks

If indeed Brazil's capital-goods sector has attained reasonable degrees of competitiveness vis-à-vis the international market, as the limited evidence suggests, the question must be raised why Brazil needs such high levels of net protection in the internal market, as is evident in the case where domestic production is subsidized. Such protection frequently appears excessive. Moreover, the form of providing the bulk of the protection, domestic production subsidies, seems especially insidious for two reasons. First, it is less visible than a regularly enforced tariff. Second, the domestic production subsidies are highly discretionary, extending substantital authority to policymaking officials. In fact, the unequal application of protective policy instruments across firms within an industry may very well be a more important dimension of Brazilian commercial policy than the variation of protection across industries.

Notes

1. The way in which these various policies are interrelated is developed in appendix 2A through the use of a partial-equilibrium supply-and-demand model.

2. The policies described in the study are thus those in force during the 1978-1979 period.

3. Some estimates can be found in Affonso Celso Pastore, José Roberto M. de Barros, and Décio Kadota, "Sobre a Taxa de Câmbio: Resultados Adicionais e uma Réplica à Análise de Bacha," *Pesquisa e Planejamento Econômico*, Vol. 8, No. 2 (August 1978), pp. 457-474 and Claudio R. Contador, "A Taxa Social de Câmbio," unpublished paper, 1979.

4. See Carlos von Doellinger et al., "Considerações à Política Cambial Brasileira Pós-1973," IPLAN/IPEA, unpublished paper, November 1979.

5. Marcos G. Fonseca, Akihiro Ikeda, and José Paulo Z. Chahad, *Pesquisa Complementar sobre Substituição de Importação de Bens de Capital*, FIPE, Part A, February 1978, pp. 203-204. Appendix table B-1 presents information on nominal and realized tariff rates for capital goods in 1974 according to the FIPE classification system.

6. In 1970 this industry accounted for 19 percent of total Brazilian capital goods production, more than any of the other 15 industries. IBGE, *Matriz de Relações Interindustriais: Brasil, 1970* (Rio de Janeiro: IBGE, 1976). Information published in the description of the table was used to classify the import and tariff information as reported in table 2-4, classified according to the IBGE input-output table format.

7. For the development of this argument the reader is referred to Regis Bonelli and Luiz Otávio Façanha, "A Indústria de Bens de Capital no Brasil: Desenvolvimento, Problemas e Perspectivas," in Wilson Suzigan, ed., *Industria: Política, Instituições e Desenvolvimento*, Monografia no. 28 (Rio de Janeiro: IPEA/INPES, 1978).

8. For a good discussion of the magnitude of the government's impact on the economy see Werner Baer, Isaac Kerstenetsky, and Annibal V. Villela, "The Changing Role of the State in the Brazilian Economy," *World Development*, 1, no. 11 (November 1973).

9. These figures were cited by a Planning Secretariat official in an interview.

10. The best available, up-to-date analysis of the role of CDI and overall industrial policy is contained in Wilson Suzigan, "Política Industrial no Brasil," in *Indústria: Política, Instituições e Desenvolvimento*, ed. Wilson Suzigan, Monografia no. 28 (Rio de Janeiro: IPEA/INPES, 1978).

11. A sectoral breakdown of Participation Agreements for 1977 is presented in appendix table B-2.

12. The activities qualifying for the 50 to 80 percent reductions are listed in Portaria No. 442 of August 10, 1976. It should be noted that the products to be imported are not identified, but rather the importing or using industry. For example, the production of most types of capital goods receives 80 percent reductions on import taxes. On the other hand, no consumer-goods production activity receives more than 50 percent.

13. In a well-publicized case the government firm Petrobras has received a 100 percent reduction of import taxes for a project.

14. For a development of this general theme, at least as it applied up to the mid-1960s, along with an analysis of the historical development of the Brazilian capital-goods sector, see Nathaniel H. Leff, *The Brazilian Capital Goods Industry, 1929-1964* (Cambridge, Massachusetts: Harvard University Press, 1968).

15. The legislation specifying the accelerated depreciation scheme was Decree 54,298 of September 23, 1964.

16. Actually, a fiscal credit to the purchaser of domestically produced capital goods originates with Decree Law 1137 of July 12, 1970.

17. Affonso Celso Pastore, José Augusto Arantes Savasini, and Joal de Azambuja Rosa, "Quantificação dos Incentivos ás Exportações," Fundação Centro de Estudos do Comércio Exterior, Rio de Janeiro, 1977, unpublished manuscript.

18. FINAME, *Relatório Anual*, 1977.

19. For a period, FINAME credits were extended with so-called prefixed monetary correction of 20 percent, which, in effect, was a ceiling imposed on the monetary correction. This practice, leading to considerable credit subsidization, has been discontinued on FINAME lending, according to an official spokesman.

20. Total loan approvals for the capital-goods producing industries by BNDE long-term lending arrangements and by EMBRAMEC totaled Cr $3.4 billion in 1976, as compared to FINAME special program commitments of Cr $17.0 for that year.

21. See, among others, Bela Balassa et al., *The Structure of Protection in Developing Countries* (Baltimore: Johns Hopkins University Press, 1971).

22. Paulo Neuhaus and Helenamaria Lobato, "Proteção Efetiva à Indústria no Brasil, 1973-1975," Fundação Centro de Estudos do Comércio Exterior, Rio de Janeiro, 1978, unpublished manuscript.

23. An explanation of the estimating procedure employed is provided in appendix 2B.

24. For the Industrial Equipment and Machinery Industry, the relevant technical coefficient for all steel inputs was 0.098. IBGE, *Matriz de Relações Interindustriais: Brasil 1970*. (Rio de Janeiro: IBGE, 1976), p. 2-2.

25. While international prices reflect the disordered present situation in the world steel market, a recent study has presented some evidence indicating that for some basic steel items Brazilian prices do not compare unfavorably with the *domestic* market prices for the major steel-exporting countries. See Instituto Brasileiro de Siderurgia, "O Preço dos Laminados de Aço no Brasil e no Exterior: Estudo Comparativo," Comissão Técnica de Economia, unpublished report, June 1977.

26. Our measure of net protection (p_j) can be written as

$$p_j = (P_{Mj}/P_{Dj})/\theta_j$$

where P_{Mj} = the effective purchase price of imported product j,
P_{Dj} = the effective purchase price of domestically produced project j,
θ = coefficient of distortion.

27. The Law of the National Similar applies only to imports which are included under an official investment program, enjoying the benefit of government investment incentives. Imports can be undertaken without the CACEX examination of national similarity if there are no government incentives involved. In other words, despite all the attention given to the Law of the National Similar, the latter has no protective teeth unless some government incentive scheme is involved.

28. This 30 percent figure is consistent with recent estimates employing either the Bacha-Taylor or UNIDO procedures. See Claudio R. Contador, "A Taxa Social de Câmbio," unpublished paper, 1979.

29. This measure equals the ratio of the estimates in table 2-8's columns (4) and (5), divided by the coefficient of distortion in column (8).

30. The protection on inputs is clearly a policy variable. Dismantling this protection would result, *ceteris paribus*, in an increase in net protection afforded the capital goods industries. Likewise, a real depreciation of the cruzeiro would have similar effects.

31. Suely Barbosa Monnerat, "Comércio Externo na Área de Bens de Capital-Periods: 1973-76," EMBRAMEC, unpublished report, November 1977.

32. See appendix table B-3 for estimates of the export subsidies for the capital goods industries.

33. Alternatively, this can be seen by comparing column (6) of table 2-8 with 1 minus the estimates given in column (3) of appendix table B-3.

34. See chapter 4.

35. EMBRAMEC, "Competitividade da Indústria Brasileira de Bens de Capital," unpublished paper, 1978.

Appendix 2A: Some Conceptual Notes on Protection of the Capital-Goods Industry

The system of protection and incentives for the capital-goods industry in Brazil involves three major elements: import restrictions in the form of implicit quotas, tariffs in conjunction with an import deposit, and subsidies and tax rebates for some domestically produced capital goods. This system of protection, which is administratively highly elaborate, is counterbalanced by other economic policies having the effect of disprotecting the capital-goods industry: exchange-rate overvaluation, and protection for inputs into the domestic capital-goods industry. The purpose of these notes is to separate analytically and to demonstrate the interaction of the three components of protection, as currently exercised for the capital-goods industry. For this purpose, a partial-equilibrium supply-and-demand model is used.

Begin by assuming a market for a given type of capital equipment, as represented by figure 2A-1. Further, assume that Brazil cannot affect international prices for the product. Therefore, the world price (P_w, in dollars) can be depicted in domestic currency as either an infinitely elastic supply or demand curve ($P_w \cdot r$), where (r) is the cruzeiro-dollar exchange rate. Since the world price is expressed in domestic currency units, changes in the cruzeiro-dollar exchange rate amount to shifts in the curve $P_w \cdot r$. Given $P_w \cdot r$ in figure 2A-1, the absence of additional restrictions or trade would imply imports of *AB*, domestic production of *OA* and the market price of $P_w \cdot r$. A devaluation, that is, an increase in r, would decrease imports, increase domestic production, and increase the domestic price level.

Now consider the introduction of a quota on imports. As reflected in references to nationalization indexes for capital-goods purchases for industrial development projects as approved by the CDI or other official agencies, the government decides to permit the entry of a certain level of imports of the capital good in question without the payment of import taxes.[1] Suppose the amount decided upon, in a piecemeal decision procedure, is equal to the amount *AC* in figure 2A-1. This has the effect of shifting the domestic supply curve for the product at a price above $P_w \cdot r$ from S_0S_0 to $S_0'S_0'$. The amount *AC* is imported at the international price P_w and costs purchasers $P_w \cdot r$ per unit. For amounts greater than *OC* in the market the domestic supply curve $S_0'S_0'$ is relevant.

Assume, as in the Brazilian case, the implicit quota is supplemented by a tariff, amounting to tariff rate t (currently around 40 percent for most capital goods). The tariff serves to bring about a new domestic price which

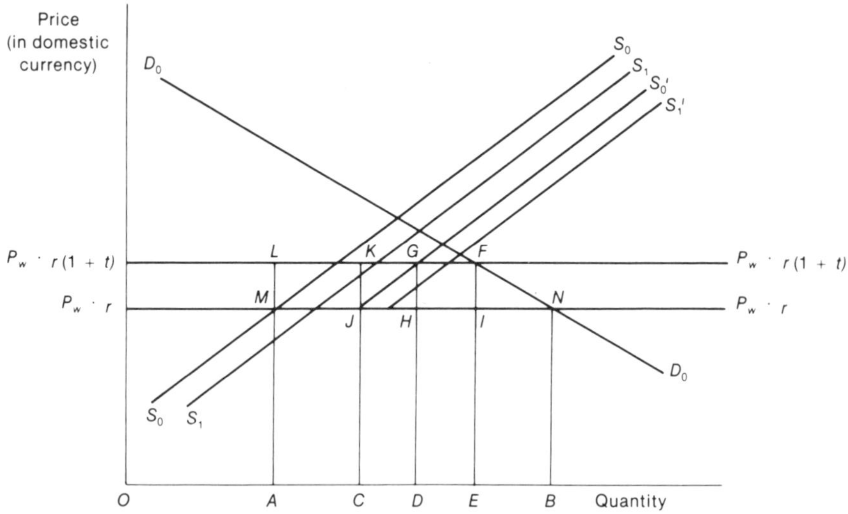

Figure 2A-1. Partial Equilibrium Trade Model with Distortions

is equivalent to $P_w \cdot r\,(1+t)$. This is equal to the constant import price with the tariff under the existing exchange rate *r*. Domestic production is equal to *OA* plus *CD*, while imports are represented by *AC* (under the quota) plus *DE* (under the tariff).

With the combined tariff and quota system, the actual tariff revenue collected amounts to the tariff rate *t* times the dutiable imports. Thus, the rectangle *GFIH* depicts the actual tariffs collected. Depending upon the amount of the imports exempted from the tariff, the actual tariffs collected relative to total imports *AC* plus *DE* will be smaller than implied by the nominal tariff rate *t*. Actual tariff collections divided by total imports (*GFIH* divided by the sum of rectangles *DEIH* plus *ACJM*) gives a misleading notion as to tariff protection and the difference between international and domestic prices. The ratio of tariff collections to total imports has no economic meaning other than to reflect the extent to which imports come under tariff-exempt schemes (that is, implicit quotas). Nevertheless, these ratios have been employed in a number of recent studies of protection in Brazil.[2]

If tariffs were charged on the imports *AC* the tariffs collected on these imports would have been equal to *MJKL*. Instead, this amount represents a transfer (subsidy) to purchasers. Since there is no practical resale for equipment imported under an officially approved project, it is a subsidy on the use of imported capital equipment. Since this effectively lowers the cost of capital goods for the investor, the choice of technology for industrial projects may be affected.

The amounts *JHG* and *INF* represent deadweight losses for society. For a program of protection to be economically justifiable over time, these social welfare losses must necessarily be more than offset by gains obtained through shifts in the domestic production supply function downward and outward as domestic producers acquire greater productive efficiency and/or economies of scale.

Under the protection scheme so far developed, it can be seen that a reduction in the allowable imports under the quota, done by tightening up the expected "nationalization index" for capital-goods purchases under approved projects, will not bring about fewer total imports. Rather it means that the reduced imports under the implicit quota arrangements will be equaled by an increase in the imports effected under the tariff. The subsidy to the capital-goods users (the rectangle *MJKL*) is reduced and an exactly offsetting gain is registered for government tariff revenues. This result is the same if tariff reductions, instead of exemptions, are employed.

As actually administered by CACEX authorities, the granting of tariff exemptions, along with other border tax exemptions, is not unrelated to the tariff rate. The decision as to whether to allow the importation of the products with the tariff exemption or to force the purchaser to buy domestically produced equipment instead is frequently based on a comparative price consideration. If the investor can show that the price of the domestically produced good is greater than the international price plus the tariff, he is generally permitted to import the product with the tariff exemption (reduction).

The third element of the Brazilian protection and incentive scheme for the capital-goods industry is the subsidies to domestic production. These subsidies take several forms. First, in addition to exempting the payment of the industrial product tax (IPI) and the state value-added tax (ICM) for the purchase of domestically produced equipment, an officially approved project allows the producing firm to use accumulated tax credits to settle other tax liabilities.[3] This amounts to a subsidy and is identical to the fiscal subsidies allowed producers of manufactured exports. An additional fiscal subsidy is administered through an accelerated depreciation allowance for domestically produced capital equipment. Credit subsidies constitute a third form of subsidy afforded to domestic capital-goods producers.

Analytically, these forms of subsidies for domestic capital-goods production can be treated as a shift of the domestic supply function. Production and sales costs are lowered through the subsidies. In terms of figure 2A-1, assume the combined magnitude of the subsidies serves to shift the domestic supply curve from S_0S_0 to S_1S_1. Assume that the amount of imports allowed under the implicit quota scheme remains unchanged, that is, still equal to the amount *AC*, so that $S_1'S_1'$ corresponds to $S_0'S_0'$.

The effect of the subsidies will be to expand domestic production at the expense of imports under the tariff. Depending upon the size of the shift downward in the domestic supply curve due to the production subsidy, it is possible to imagine there being a complete elimination of imports under the tariff. This could be seen by a slightly further shift in S_1S_1, and correspondingly in $S_1'S_1'$. If $S_1'S_1'$ were to intersect with the demand schedule D_0D_0 beyond point F there would be pressure downward on the domestic price, and the tariff would become redundant (and prohibitive).[4] In this case the imports brought in under the quota system would undoubtedly attract the increasing attention of protection-minded domestic producers. Decreasing the quota (via insistence on higher nationalization indexes for the equipment component in approved industrial projects) would serve to increase domestic production and bolster the market price.

Notes

1. Actually, under present circumstances, it is only rarely that *full* exemptions are granted. The exemptions are generally given for 50 to 80 percent of the import and border taxes. As such they are reductions rather than exemptions. These modifications in the recent protection arrangements, however, do not alter the general content of our analysis. They simply reduce the transfer to importers.

2. See Paulo Neuhaus and Helenamaria Lobato, "Proteção Efetiva à Indústria no Brasil, 1973-1975," Fundação Centro de Estudos do Comércio Exterior, Rio de Janeiro, unpublished manuscript, 1978. See also, Affonso Celso Pastore et al., "Análise da Promoção de Exportações sob a Ótica da Proteção Efetiva, Fundação Centro de Estudos do Comércio Exterior, Rio de Janeiro, unpublished manuscript, 1977.

3. These fiscal incentives for domestically produced capital goods were enacted in July 1974 with Decree Law 1335.

4. Because of market imperfections, product heterogeneity (either perceived or real), and delivery scheduling difficulties, some imports under the tariff may still occur. In the case of tariff redundancy neither the nominal tariff rate nor the realized tariff rate would be a meaningful measure of the difference between domestic and international prices.

Appendix 2B: Notes on the Measurement of Protection

Introduction

In order to assess quantitatively the effects of economic policies on the relative profitability of imported and domestically produced capital goods, a measure of net protection has been developed. Our measure, which we will call the index of net protection, differs from the concepts of either effective protection or domestic resource costs in that it focuses on the unit profitability of domestic production as affected by various economic policies. Ad hoc comparisons are made between the prices of domestically produced and imported goods as they are affected by different policies.

While the standard measures of effective protection and domestic resource costs must take into account the differences between domestic and international prices, both employ observed differences. This is satisfactory if the differences can be accurately observed. In the great body of the empirical work, however, the observed differences between domestic and international prices are taken to be the prevailing tariff levels. Even in the case of protection solely by tariffs, the tariffs may possess some degree of redundancy, and consequently the prevailing tariffs will not accurately reflect the difference between international and domestic prices. In the event of subsidies, import deposits, and other nontariff barriers, tariff information alone, of course, will give inappropriate indications of protection. Alternative measures of price differences must be employed. As anyone who has dealt with protection is aware, actual price comparisons, while ideal, are difficult to undertake, especially if aggregation is necessary.

Our measure of protection focuses on *possible* differences between domestic and import prices instead of the (inadequately) *observed* differences. This procedure appears more suitable in the case of a plethora of nontariff barriers to imports. Moreover, our measure can provide a better overall indication of the range of net protection when there are alternative schemes for the same products, which is frequently the case when a combination of tariffs, quotas, and subsidies is provided.

Measurement Techniques

Our measure of net protection p is an index involving two distinct components. We can write:

$$p_j = \frac{\tau_j}{\theta_j} \tag{2A.1}$$

where τ_j represents an index of nominal, direct protection for product *j* and, θ_j is equal to a coefficient of distortion. Tariff protection, border taxes, port and maritime charges, import deposits, financial subsidies, fiscal subsidies and quota arrangements are all reflected in τ_j. These policies directly affect the profitability of domestic producers vis-à-vis foreign producers. The coefficient of distortion θ_j, on the other hand, reflects exchange rate policy and protection of the inputs used to product product *j*.

If there is no nominal, direct protection, no exchange-rate distortions, and free trade in product *j*'s inputs, the index of net protection would be equal to 1.0. To the extent that there is net protection through economic policies, the index p_j would be greater than 1.0. A value of p_j, for example, of 1.4 would indicate a 40 percent level of net protection for domestic producers relative to their *ex factory* price. If p_j is less than 1.0, the production process for product *j* is negatively protected by economic policies.

Looking first at the coefficient of distortion θ_j, the concept is intended to reflect (1) distortions in exchange-rate policy and (2) policies protecting the inputs used in the production of product *j*. Such policies protecting inputs, of course, raise their prices and serve to render the process of producing product *j* less internationally competitive. Both the distortions coming from exchange-rate overvaluation (or undervaluation) and protection of inputs must be taken into consideration in assessing the net protection for product *j*. Our coefficient of distortion θ_j is taken here to be simply the sum of the two effects, or

$$\theta_j = 1 + \frac{r^* - r}{r} + \frac{\sum_i a_{ii} t_i}{\sum_i a_{ij}} \left(\sum_1 a_{ij}\right). \tag{2A.2}$$

Simplifying, we can write

$$\theta_j = \frac{r^*}{r} + \sum_i a_{ij} t_i .$$

The term $(r^* - r)/r$ measures the amount of exchange rate overvaluation (or undervaluation, if negative), where r is the official, prevailing exchange rate and r^* is the shadow equilibrium exchange rate. The value of r^* must be estimated by making assumptions about the magnitude of capital flows, price elasticities, and possible changes in trade restrictions external to the country.

In the last term of equation 2A.2, reflecting the level of protection on inputs *i*, the a_{ij}'s represent the technical coefficients of a free trade input-output table. The variable t_i is the level of nominal protection afforded to input *i*. While all forms of protection should be included, our empirical exercises, carried out for the Brazilian capital-goods industry, had to be undertaken using realized tariff rates. The component $\Sigma_i a_{ij} t_i / \Sigma_i a_{ij}$ measures measures the level of protection on inputs. Since the sum of the inputs represents only a part of the value of the final product, the effect of protection on inputs on the price of the product *j* applies only to the portion of the final product accounted for by inputs.

The measure of nominal, direct protection τ_j is equal to the ratio of import to domestic prices available to the domestic purchaser of product *j*. It is written $\tau_j = P_{Mj}/P_{Dj}$. The buyer's import price reflects all prevailing tariff restrictions, import deposits, border taxes, and other surcharges levied on top of the CIF import price valued at the official exchange rate. The buyer's price of the domestically produced product *j* likewise reflects indirect taxes and the effects of any fiscal and/or financial subsidies. The point of departure for the analysis of the effects of all such policies on nominal, direct protection is that the CIF import price at the official exchange rate and the *ex factory,* nonsubsidized domestic price are equal. The further assumptions are that the possible buyer prices of imports and domestic production reflect the prevailing policies, and that consumer choice is a function of relative prices. Discounting foreign freight changes, the costs of production of the foreign and domestic product are held to be the same for the purposes of analyzing the price effects of policies. The question is to what extent do policies favor or disfavor the domestic producer.

The price of the imported product *j* payable by the purchaser can be written as:

$$P_{Mj} = P_{MCIFj} + (1\text{-}\alpha)t_j P_{MCIFj} + (1\text{-}\alpha)t_{IPIj}\,[P_{MCIFj} + (1\text{-}\alpha)t_j P_{MCIFj}] + (1\text{-}\alpha)t_{ICM} \quad P_{MCIFj} + (1\text{-}\alpha)t_j P_{MCIFj} + (1\text{-}\alpha)t_{IPIj}\,[P_{MCIFj} + (1\text{-}\alpha)t_j P_{MCIFj}] \quad + t_p P_{MFOBj} + \beta\, P_{MFOBj}\,(i\text{-}i_{CB}) \tag{2A.3}$$

where

P_{MCIFj} = CIF import price for product *j*,
P_{MFOBj} = FOB import price for product *j*,
α = exemption proportion for payment of tariffs, IPI and ICM taxes under approved government programs,

t_j = nominal tariff rate for product j,
t_{IPIj} = IPI tax rate for product j,
t_{ICM} = ICM tax rate,
t_p = rate for port taxes, including port improvement tax, merchant marine tax, and storage and brokerage fees (estimated as 0.06 of P_{MFOB}),
β = proportion of FOB import price required as a prior import deposit, currently 100 percent held for one year,
i = nominal effective market interest rate,
i_{CB} = nominal effective interest rate paid on advance import deposits, currently set at zero.

The parameter α, denoting the extent of tax reduction, is not product-specific. Rather, it varies from transaction to transaction depending upon approval of the import as part of an official investment project. In the case of a 100-percent tariff and tax reduction, the term (1-α) takes on a value of zero.

The CIF import price is greater than the FOB import price by the amount of freight and insurance charges. We can write

$$P_{MCIFj} = P_{MFOBj} + \phi P_{MFOBj} \tag{2A.4}$$

where ϕ represents the shipping charges expressed as a proportion of the FOB import price. Observation indicates that ϕ varies slightly over products and is equal to about 0.15. Solving equation 2A.4 for P_{MFOBj} and substituting in equation 2A.3, factoring out P_{MCIFj} and simplifying, we obtain

$$P_{Mj} = P_{MCIFj}\{1 + (1\text{-}\alpha)t_j + (1\text{-}\alpha)t_{IPIj}[1 + (1\text{-}\alpha)t_j] + (1\text{-}\alpha)t_{ICM}\ \{1 + (1\text{-}\alpha)t_j + (1\text{-}\alpha)t_{IPIj}[1 + (1\text{-}\alpha)t_j]\} + \frac{t_p}{1+\phi} + \frac{\beta(i\text{-}i_{CB})}{1+\phi}\} \tag{2A.5}$$

The domestic purchase price of the domestically produced product j is likewise affected by direct commercial policies. It is written as

$$P_{Dj} = P_{Fj} + (1\text{-}\gamma)\, t_{IPIj}P_{Fj} + (1\text{-}\gamma)t_{ICMj}\,(P_{Fj} + t_{IPIj}\ P_{Fj}) - \gamma s_{IPIj}P_{Fj} - d_jP_{Fj} - \left[1 - \left(\frac{i'}{i}\right)\frac{(1 - \frac{1}{(1\text{-}i)^n})}{(1 - \frac{1}{(1+i')^n})}\right]P_{Fj} \tag{2A.6}$$

where

P_{Fj} = domestic factory price for product j,
γ = proportion of IPI and ICM taxes which are exempted for a domestically produced product, currently either 1 or 0,
t_{IPIj} = IPI tax rate applied to product j,
t_{ICMj} = ICM tax rate applied to product j,
s_{IPIj} = fiscal subsidy element for product j operating through accumulated IPI and ICM tax credits,
d_j = proportional effect of accelerated depreciation allowance for purchaser on potential price,
i' = nominal effective interest rate charged on loans as a part of official credit programs (for example, FINAME) for purchasing product j,
i = nominal effective market interest rate,
n = term of loan (years).

The last term in equation 2A.6 represents the change in the competitive domestic price which is possible as a result of official, subsidized credit programs for purchasers. Factoring out P_{Fj}, we have

$$P_{Dj} = P_{Fj} \quad 1 + (1\text{-}\gamma)t_{IPIj} + (1\text{-}\gamma)t_{ICMj}(1 + t_{IPIj}) - \gamma s_{IPIj}$$

$$- d_j - \left[1 - \frac{(\frac{i'}{i}).1 - \frac{1}{(1+i)^n}}{1 - \frac{1}{(1+i')^n}} \right] \qquad \text{(2A-7)}$$

Since for the purposes of analyzing the direct effect of policies, P_{MCIFj} P_{Fj} are assumed to be equal, the measure of nominal direct protection τ_j can be calculated as the ratio of the expressions within the brackets of equations 2A.5 and 2A.7.

3 The Development of Small-Scale Industry

Introduction: Economic Setting

The key to Brazilian economic growth in the past twenty years has been rapid industrial expansion. During that period industrial output has increased by an annual average of about 9 percent. This industrial growth has been fostered by the Brazilian government through a myriad of commercial, credit, and fiscal policies, along with direct governmental productive activity in a few key sectors such as electric energy, chemicals, and steel. Although not explicit, the emphasis in policy has been on large industrial operations. Substantial resources have been marshalled in the formation of public industrial firms, and the operations of these firms, without exception, have been large-scale, once established. Another dimension of the Brazilian industrialization strategy has been to create a hospitable environment for transnational firms; to encourage their establishment and increased output in Brazil. Like the public firms, transnational firms tend to be large. In addition to an implicit emphasis on public and transnational firm activities, the effect of industrial policy, operating through various government programs, has been to promote large-scale enterprises. Those firms best organized and equipped to take advantage of the incentive programs have tended to be large enterprises.

The economic effects of Brazilian industrial policies have been well documented.[1] Besides promoting impressive industrial growth, numerous distortions have resulted. Relatively little labor absorption has occurred in manufacturing, and the industrial sector which has emerged after a period of continuing intense industrial growth is relatively capital-intensive. The much debated, observed increased inequality in relative income shares in part must be seen as a reflection of the type of industrialization pursued. Clearly, the emphasis on large capital-intensive industrial projects and enterprises has exacerbated the situation.

That small and medium-sized enterprises (SME) have been largely bypassed by Brazilian industrialization policy has gradually come to be recognized in many governmental quarters. To offset the bias in favor of large-scale enterprise, a number of specific programs for SME have been in-

---

itiated in recent years. Aside from some special credit programs, to be discussed in a later section of this chapter, the main expression of governmental concern for the problems and role of SME has been the establishment of CEBRAE (Centro de Brasileiro de Apoio à Pequena e Média Empresa).

This chapter begins by discussing the role of SME in the Brazilian economy, examining SME participation in total industrial value added and employment. Sectoral, as well as regional, differences between SME and large enterprises will be analyzed along with differences in productivity and capital intensity. In the following section, attention will be devoted to the performance of SME over time. The reasons for success and failure are then treated separately, examining the problems evident with SME in Brazil. The next section will concentrate on the existing institutional arrangements for providing financing to Brazilian SME, followed by a summary and concluding remarks.

The definition of SME is necessarily an arbitrary one. In Brazil various definitions exist. While a "micro" enterprise is commonly thought of as one having less than 10 employees, exactly what constitutes a "small," or "medium," sized enterprise is subject to a wide range of operational and other interpretations, employing different types of criteria. For example, for the Central Bank an SME is one having annual sales up to 85,000 times a standard reference value (MVR) equal to Cr/$1,150.70 in 1978; in June 1978 this meant that a firm with annual sales up to U.S. $5.5 million qualified as an SME.[2] The National Development Bank (BNDE) considers an SME as any establishment having fixed assets plus the projected investment of up to 500,000 times the value of the readjustable treasury bond (ORTN), which bond was equal to Cr $263 in June 1978. Thus, to qualify for BNDE as an SME the firm's fixed assets plus intended investments could total up to U.S $7.5 million. CEBRAE, while employing both criteria involving sales and employment totals, has maintained a more operationally flexible definition by stressing qualitative criteria such as the organization of the firm, market conditions, and the relationship between owner and employees. Recognizing the importance of sectoral differences, CEBRAE has sought to be pragmatic in its provision of assistance to SME. It should be noted, however, that in general what constitutes an SME for CEBRAE is much smaller than that for either the Central Bank or BNDE.

For the purpose of our analysis we will employ a definitional criterion widely used by Brazilian observers analyzing official census data. An enterprise is considered small if it employs less than 100 persons, medium sized if it employs between 100 and 249 individuals, and large if it employs more than 250 persons. An alternative definition could just as easily have been chosen; the results of the analysis, however, would not differ appreciably in their import.

Participation of SME in Brazilian Manufacturing

The primary statistical sources for analyzing the participation of SME in the Brazilian industrial sector are the industrial censuses undertaken by IBGE. The most recent available census information is for 1970.[3] Table 3-1 summarizes the participation as small, medium, and large enterprises in total Brazilian manufacturing.[4] As to be expected, small firms account for the lion's share of the total number of manufacturing enterprises. In 1970 nearly 98 percent of all such enterprises employed less than 100 individuals.

In terms of either total output or value added, small firms were also seen to be significant. In 1970, 36 percent of all manufacturing value added was provided by small enterprises. It is clear, however, that large enterprises were the most important in contributing to total output, tax collections and manufacturing value added.

Small enterprises occupy a special importance when it comes to employment generation. Table 3-1 indicates that 50 percent of all Brazilian manufacturing employment was in small enterprises in 1970. Of that amount—equal to over 1 million workers—approximately one-half was in very small enterprises—those with less than 20 employees. The conclusion of this analysis is inescapable. Small manufacturing enterprises are extremely important in providing employment in Brazil.

As seen in table 3-1, small enterprises accounted for 37 percent of the total 1970 salaries and wages paid in Brazilian manufacturing. Comparing this figure with the 50 percent share of small enterprises in manufacturing employment, it is evident that salaries and wages per worker are lower in small enterprises than in larger enterprises. Average salaries and wages have been computed for different sized establishments and are listed in the last column of table 3-1. As seen, as establishment size increases, average salaries and wages increase. In the very smallest category, that is, establishments with 1-4 workers, there is a tendency to understate actual labor remuneration because frequently the owner and his immediate family, while counted as workers if so engaged, do not actually receive wage payments. Even discounting these establishments, there is nevertheless a clear increase in average labor remuneration with increases in establishment size. This can be interpreted as an increase in skilled labor requirements accompanying an increase in establishment size. Small enterprises employ more in the way of unskilled labor than do larger enterprises. Not only do small firms employ more labor than larger establishments, but they also contribute more to absorbing Brazil's excess supply of unskilled labor.

Disaggregating the manufacturing sector by industry, there are evident some important differences. Small enterprises are much more important in some industries than others. Table 3-2 presents information on the participation of small, medium, and larger establishments in the total employ-

Table 3-1
Participation of Small, Medium, and Large Enterprises in Brazilian Manufacturing, 1970

Size of Establishment (as measured according to number of workers)	Number of Establishments (N)		Value of Production (X)		Employment[a] (L)		Salaries and Wages (W)		Taxes[b]	Value Added (VA)		Value Added per Employee (VA/L)	Average Salary per Employee (W/L)
	N	Percent	Cr$ Million	Percent	Number	Percent	Cr$ Million	Percent	Percent Total	Cr$ Million	Percent	Cr$ 000	Cr$ 000
Small													
(Total)	138,764	97.7	33,573.8	37.5	1,043,210	50.3	3,435.1	37.0	25.3	14,426.3	35.7	13.83	3.14
1-4	87,555	61.7	4,114.0	4.6	199,624	9.6	271.8	2.9	1.9	1,574.4	3.9	7.89	1.36
5-19	38,364	27.4	9,875.1	11.0	343,916	16.6	1,045.3	11.3	6.9	4,146.7	10.3	12.06	3.04
20-99	12,245	8.6	19,584.7	21.9	499,670	24.1	2,118.0	22.8	16.6	8,705.2	21.5	17.42	4.24
Medium	2,035	1.4	15,079.3	16.8	313,168	15.1	1,501.8	16.2	15.2	6,777.2	16.8	21.64	4.80
Large	1,213	0.9	40,961.6	45.7	718,533	34.6	4,339.1	46.8	59.5	19,210.1	47.5	26.74	6.04
Total[c]	142,110	100.0	89,621.9	100.0	2,074,911	100.0	9,276.0	100.0	100.0	40,486.5	100.0	19.48	4.47

Source: Special IBGE tabulations from the 1970 economic census made for CEBRAE.

[a]Includes all economically active personnel.

[b]These taxes are the ICM and IPI.

[c]The totals may differ slightly from the sums of the components due to rounding and some data omission.

Table 3-2

Participation of Small, Medium, and Large Enterprises in Total Industry Employment and Value Added, by Industry, 1970

(percent)

Industry	Establishments			Employment			Value Added		
	Small	*Medium*	*Large*	*Small*	*Medium*	*Large*	*Small*	*Medium*	*Large*
Mining	97.2	1.3	0.8	43.0	12.6	44.4	22.1	10.2	57.6
Total manufacturing	97.2	1.4	0.9	50.3	15.1	34.6	35.7	16.8	47.5
Nonmetallic minerals	99.2	0.5	0.3	69.0	8.5	12.5	39.4	13.3	27.3
Metallurgy	95.2	3.0	1.8	40.5	17.6	41.9	26.5	14.8	58.7
Machinery	94.0	3.7	2.3	39.0	19.1	39.1	39.9	19.7	40.4
Electricity and communications equipment	90.4	5.7	3.9	28.9	18.8	52.3	21.7	18.7	59.6
Transportation equipment	94.2	3.0	2.8	25.3	10.2	64.5	13.1	6.4	70.5
Lumber and wood	99.3	0.6	0.1	84.2	10.6	5.2	81.1	12.6	6.3
Furniture	99.3	0.6	0.1	81.9	11.0	7.1	72.5	15.9	10.6
Paper	89.0	7.8	3.2	37.6	25.1	37.3	30.3	25.0	45.0
Rubber	95.8	2.5	1.7	43.3	13.2	43.5	24.0	7.3	68.7
Leather	97.5	1.8	0.6	57.2	18.6	24.2	46.0	22.0	32.0
Chemicals	93.3	4.3	2.3	36.0	17.6	46.4	26.1	17.9	56.0
Drugs	86.9	6.9	5.3	31.2	21.2	47.6	21.7	27.3	50.9
Perfumery and soaps	97.0	1.9	1.0	50.8	21.5	37.7	32.2	18.8	49.0
Plastics	95.7	3.3	1.0	58.7	19.4	21.9	40.6	23.5	35.9
Textiles	88.6	5.5	5.9	23.6	15.1	61.3	28.1	14.4	57.5
Apparel and shoes	97.1	2.1	0.8	56.4	18.8	24.8	44.2	19.7	31.3
Food	98.8	0.7	0.4	61.3	15.6	23.1	52.2	21.6	26.2
Beverages	98.1	1.2	0.6	53.9	17.3	28.8	34.3	26.6	39.1
Tobacco	77.0	7.2	15.8	8.2	12.0	79.8	1.9	3.1	95.0
Printing and publishing	98.0	1.4	0.6	59.8	15.0	25.2	49.8	14.5	35.7
Miscellaneous	98.2	1.2	0.6	69.7	13.4	16.9	66.4	15.7	17.9

Source: Special IBGE tabulations from 1970 economic census made for CEBRAE.

Note: Percentages may not add up to 100 because of rounding and the omission of undeclared data.

ment and value added of twenty-one manufacturing industries. In terms of providing a large share of total industry employment, small establishments are especially important in the following industries: lumber and wood (84 percent of industry employment), furniture (81 percent), miscellaneous (70 percent), nonmetallic mineral manufacturing (60 percent), plastics (59 percent) and leather (57 percent). A similar picture emerges when the small-establishment share of industry value added is examined; the same industries possess high shares for small enterprises.

While some industries are important for having a large participation by small establishments, there are other industries, generally far more concentrated in market structure, where large firms predominate, accounting for very large shares of either total industry employment or value added. The most striking example of this is the highly concentrated tobacco industry, with 95% of the industry value added being produced in large establishments. Although less dramatic, other industries such as transportation equipment, rubber, chemicals, and electrical machinery are dominated by large establishments.

With some exceptions, the regional distribution of small, medium, and large establishments roughly parallels that for the country as a whole. It should be noted, however, that the regional distribution of manufacturing as a whole is highly concentrated geographically, with three center-south states (São Paulo, Rio de Janeiro, and Minas Gerais) accounting for 79 percent of total Brazilian manufacturing value added in 1970. The problematic and low-income northeast, an area today with an estimated 34 million inhabitants accounted for only 6 percent of Brazilian manufacturing output in 1970.[5] At the same time, however, since the northeast's share of total manufacturing establishments is larger than its share of manufacturing output or employment, the establishments in the northeast tend to be smaller on the average.

Table 3-3 is a counterpart of table 3-1 that has been prepared for analysis of the participation of small, medium, and larger manufacturing establishments in the northeast. Three northeastern states have been selected—Pernambuco, Bahia, and Ceará. Together these three most-industrialized northeastern states accounted for 76 percent of total northeastern manufacturing value added in 1972—but for only 4 percent of the national total. In the three selected northeastern states, small establishments demonstrated shares of employment and value added similar to the national totals. As seen, small establishments, accounted for 98 percent of total establishments, 50 percent of employment, 39 percent of total production value, 24 percent of taxes collected, and 37 percent of value added.

Comparing tables 3-1 and 3-3 it is evident that average manufacturing salaries are lower in the northeast than for the country as a whole. In addition to indicating some differences in labor market conditions between regions, the average wage disparity suggests a product composition favoring less skilled labor usage in the northeast. Table 3-4 examines the extent to

Table 3-3
Participation of Small, Medium, and Large Enterprises in Manufacturing for Three Northeastern States, 1970

Size of Establishment (As Measured by Number of Workers)	Number of Establishments (N)		Value of Production (X)		Employment[a] (L)		Salaries and Wages (W)			Taxes	Value Added (VA)		Value Added per Employee (VA/L)	Average Salary per Employee[c] (W/L)
	N	Percent	Cr$ Million	Percent	Number	Percent	Cr$ Million	Percent	N_w	Percent Total	Cr$ Million	Percent	Cr$ 000	Cr$ 000
Small														
(Total)	15,294	98.0	2,227.3	39.2	91,724	50.3	185.6	33.5	11,753	23.8	884.3	37.1	9.64	2.63
1-4	10,448	66.9	278.6	4.9	25,817	14.1	19.2	3.5	7,054	1.3	117.2	4.9	4.54	1.10
5-19	4,032	25.8	746.1	13.1	35,592	17.9	59.7	10.8	3,876	6.2	296.0	12.4	9.08	1.91
20-99	814	5.2	1,202.6	21.2	33,315	18.3	106.7	19.2	823	16.3	471.7	19.8	14.16	3.17
Medium	195	1.2	1,151.8	20.3	26,873	14.8	109.3	19.7	170	16.5	446.9	18.7	16.63	4.66
Large	99	.6	2,305.0	40.5	63,695	34.9	259.6	46.8	99	59.7	1,052.2	44.1	16.52	4.08
Total[d]	15,609	100.0	5,684.1	100.0	182,292	100.0	554.7	100.0	12,022	100.0	238,414	100.0	13.08	3.95

Source: Special IBGE tabulations from the 1970 economic census made for CEBRAE.

[a]Includes all economically active personnel.

[b]These taxes are the ICM and IPI.

[c]Since the sample size for employment and salaries differed, an adjustment was made to reflect the average for the size group. The resultant average salary was computed as $W/L \cdot N/N_w$.

[d]The totals may differ slightly from the sums of the components due to rounding and some data omission.

which the regional wage differences reflect a product mix phenomenon. Focusing on the three most important manufacturing industries in the northeast—food products, textiles, and apparel—it can be seen that the average wages for Brazil are still considerably higher than for the northeast. Even in the northeast, however, small establishments pay lower average wages than larger establishments, indicating that also in the northeast small enterprises employ proportionally more unskilled labor.

The question of capital intensity for small versus large enterprises is one of direct relevance to any lending program designed to promote SME. The normal contention is that small firms are less capital-intensive than larger firms and that therefore the capital cost per job created via an investment program for SME is lower than it would be in the case of larger enterprise investments.[6] Such is the case for Brazil. The analysis is rendered somewhat precarious because of the absence of reliable fixed assets data in the industrial census. First, to analyze the factor intensity of small, medium, and large sized establishments a proxy for fixed capital assets has necessarily been employed. It can be noted in both tables 3-1 and 3-3 that the ratio of value added to employees increases with the size of establishments. This ratio, indicative of labor productivity, reflects the use of capital on the part of individual establishments. The greater the use of capital, on a per worker basis, the greater the value added per employee.[7] Thus the differences in value added per employee between small and larger establishments, for both Brazil and the three northeastern states, indicate that small establishments are less capital-intensive than larger establishments. In both cases—Brazil and the northeast—the ratio *VA/L* for large establishments is nearly twice as high as for small establishments. Nothing definite about total factoral productivity or technical efficiency can be concluded from the measure of value added per employee. A firm employing much in the way of capital, as expressed by a high *VA/L* ratio, may nevertheless display a low productivity in the use of its capital. In the very small establishments, that is, those with one to four workers, the value added per employee was even lower. It should be noted further that in the northeast manufacturing in general is less capital-intensive than for the entire country.

Second, to arrive at some current estimates as to the investment cost per job created two different approaches were followed. The first procedure involved the fitting of values to an assumed production function possessing a Cobb-Douglas functional form. This procedure requires: (1) the specification of the Cobb-Douglas functional form for the production function,[8] (2) profit maximizing behavioral assumptions on the part of firms, (3) observations concerning the parameter values of the production function for small manufacturing enterprises, and (4) observations concerning factor prices. This procedure is outlined, along with the necessary assumptions, in appendix 3A. Although a range of estimates of the fixed capital cost

Table 3-4
Comparison of Value Added per Employee and Average Wages between Brazil and Three Northeastern States for the Food Products, Textiles, and Apparel Industries, 1970
(Cr $ 000)

	Value Added per Employee		*Average Wages*	
Industry and Size	*Brazil*	*Three Northeastern States*	*Brazil*	*Three Northeastern States*
Food Products				
Small	15.15	9.16	2.39	1.88
1- 4 employees	10.79	5.51	1.39	1.20
5-19 employees	14.24	9.84	2.38	1.77
20-99 employees	21.39	15.16	3.63	2.46
Medium	24.62	15.64	3.79	3.40
Large	20.34	12.16	3.73	2.60
Textiles				
Small	16.97	18.38	3.65	2.37
1- 4 employees	10.73	4.75	1.85	1.35
5-19 employees	15.91	24.44	3.25	2.38
20-99 employees	17.79	18.01	3.94	2.43
Medium	13.60	8.27	3.92	2.07
Large	13.36	9.45	3.66	3.06
Apparel				
Small	9.62	5.98	2.92	2.18
1- 4 employees	7.56	3.65	1.57	1.59
5-19 employees	8.91	5.15	2.81	1.59
20-99 employees	10.49	8.95	3.28	2.29
Medium	11.62	8.70	3.49	2.71
Large	13.97	13.59	3.34	2.57

Source: Special IBGE tabulations from the 1970 economic census made for CEBRAE.
Note: The three Northeastern states are Pernambuco, Bahia and Ceará. These are the largest and most economically important states.

per job created in small enterprises was generated, our best estimate using this procedure is around U.S. $4,000 per job created. This should be considered an average, as there are likely to be sectoral differences.

The second approach in estimating the fixed capital cost of each job created is to examine the observed results of existing SME lending programs in Brazil. In this regard, two separate strands of evidence were examined. First, the bank of the northeast's (BNB) Program of Financing for Small and Medium Industry has been in operation since 1967, during which time it has extended loans involving investments of Cr $1,745 million (in 1977 prices) in some 958 lending operations. An estimated 13,982 new jobs were created by these loans. Accordingly, it has been estimated that the average cost of a new job created through this program has been Cr $125,000 (in December 1977 prices), or approximately U.S. $7,800.[9] There are two difficulties apparent with this estimate. The investment cost is overstated since the numerator includes working capital as well as fixed capital. On the other hand, the estimate of employment generated (in the denominator) is probably overstated. This information was pro forma data supplied by the borrower at the time a loan application was made. The tendency in such cases is to exaggerate the expected increase in employment for the borrowing firm.

A second strand of evidence from lending programs relating to the capital cost of job creation in SSE is from CEBRAE-affiliated financing programs for micro enterprises. An analysis of two such programs in the very disparate states of Rio Grande de Sul and Piauí revealed average lending costs per job created in 1977 of Cr $40,000 and Cr $39,000, respectively. This amounted to approximately U.S. $2,500 per job. This figure considers only the investment made by the borrowing firm and not the administrative lending costs incurred by the lending agency or technical assistance affiliates. Moreover, since the U.S. $2,500 figure is for micro enterprises, it can reasonably be expected that the fixed capital costs per job created for small enterprises in general will be somewhat higher. Looking at these programs and the BNB program estimates in conjunction with those we made from the production function analysis, the latter best estimate (U.S. $4,000) appears to be both consistant and reasonable.

The Growth of Small and Medium-Sized Enterprise

The past 25 years in Brazil has been a period of substantial economic growth. As noted, the industrial sector has spurred such growth. Accordingly, it is logical to expect that manufacturing firms have expanded, their numbers increased, and their productivity grown. Whether or not different sized firms experience similar growth performances, however, is another question. To examine the performance of small, medium, and large establishments over time in Brazil a comparison has been made between the 1950 and 1970 industrial censuses. The basic results of this comparison are presented in table 3-5. The total number of industrial enterprises increased by 74 percent during the period. Since the number of small enterprises increased by about the same percentage (73 percent) their share of the total number of industrial enterprises remained roughly the same. Medium-sized enterprises grew the most rapidly over the 1950-1970 period, suggesting in part that some of the small enterprises grew into medium-sized establishments.[10]

The growth of industrial employment in Brazil between 1950 and

Table 3-5
Percentage Growth of Small, Medium, and Large Industrial Enterprises, 1950-1970
(percent)

Size[a]	*Number of Establishments*	*Employment*	*Value Added*[b]	*Value Added per Establishment*	*Value Added per Employee*
Small	73.2	72.5	85.4	7.0	7.5
Medium	95.3	94.2	172.7	39.6	40.3
Large	67.3	53.2	144.4	46.1	59.6
Total	73.7	73.0	127.6	31.1	31.6

Source: Computations based upon IBGE data as published in the industrial censuses.

[a]Small, medium and large establishments were classified as follows:

Small: 1-99 persons employed

Medium: 100-499 persons employed

Large: more than 500 persons employed.

[b]Current price value added data were deflated by the wholesale industrial price index. Although this procedure has somewhat understated the growth of real value added, the understatement has affected the small, medium, and large size categories in the same way. Therefore, the observed relative changes among categories are unaffected by an understatement of real income growth.

1970 was 74 percent, as seen in table 3-5. For small enterprises the proportional growth was the same, indicating no change in their share of total industrial employment. The greatest observed absolute employment growth occurred in medium-sized establishments.

Examining value added growth, the disparities are more uneven. As in the case of employment and the number of establishments, medium-sized establishments enjoyed the greatest absolute increase in value added—173 percent between 1950 and 1970. Yet, in terms of value added per establishment it was the largest establishments which registered the greatest gains—46 percent as opposed to 40 percent for medium-sized establishments. On the other hand, growth in value added per establishment for small establishments was quite modest during the period—only 7 percent.

In great part the slow growth in value added per establishment for small enterprises reflects their slow growth in labor productivity. Value added per employee for small establishments grew by only 7.5 percent for the entire 1950-1970 period. This suggests little in the way of capital deepening took place for small firms. These firms have remained labor-intensive. On the other hand, labor productivity grew significantly in medium and large establishments. In the latter, the twenty-year growth in value added per employee was 60 percent, equal to a simple annual average growth rate of 3 percent. This suggests an increase in capital intensity, especially in large establishments.

What can explain the observed disparities in growth of small and larger establishments over time? In great part, the answer lies in the economic policies pursued by the Brazilian government over the past 25 years. Economic policy has favored the growth and establishment of large firms and has essentially, although to a great degree inadvertently, discriminated against SSEs. This inherent discrimination can be seen in several ways.

First, the industries promoted by Brazilian economic policy, along import-substitution lines, have been those which tend to be universally the most concentrated and in general the least suitable for SSE. Responding to differential incentives and resource pulls introduced by economic policy, the composition of Brazilian industrial output has changed in favor of those industries where SSE's tend to be least important. The highest rates of industrial growth during the last 25 years have been witnessed in metallurgy, electrical machinery and communications equipment, transportation equipment, chemicals, rubber, drugs, and machinery.[11] In other countries, as well as in Brazil, these industries appear to be the least conducive to SSE activities.[12] Industrial strategy has promoted the rapid growth of these industries over the last 25 years. These rapid growth industries are also those where public firms and transnational corporations have exercised their greatest role and where such firms tend to account for large shares of output and output growth. As noted previously, these firms tend to be large.

Industries which possess a higher participation of small enterprises with respect to value added and employment have tended to grow slower. These industries include food products, apparel and footwear, furniture, lumber, printing and publishing, and nonmetallic mineral manufacturing. By and large, import substitution in these industries had been complete by 1950, implying that further increases in demand had come either from domestic market expansion or exports. The domestic market did not grow dramatically for the products of these industries, and manufactured exports were discriminated against rather substantially until the late 1960s. Had the constellation of economic policy been more open (that is, export oriented) in the 1950s and early 1960s, the composition of industrial output would have most certainly undergone a change more conducive to SSE activities. Brazil possesses a natural comparative advantage in lumber and wood products, leather goods, furniture, apparel and footwear, and many food products, and these industries display a large participation on the part of SSE.

Second, in addition to looking at the overall industrialization strategy and the resultant change in Brazil's industrial output composition, individual policies can also be examined and shown to be discriminatory against SSE. One commonly used policy instrument to spur industrial development has been fiscal incentives. A firm's tax liability is reduced if the firm engages in designated practices such as investment in certain indicated activities or geographical regions. By and large, SSE's do not have the administrative ability to take advantage of such programs, nor do they possess sufficient size to render the tax breaks in fact attractive.

Aside from commercial and exchange policies, *a la* protection, affecting the relative profitability in different sectors and therefore the distribution of investable resources, the main policy instrument by which industrial investment itself has been promoted has been credit incentives and subsidies. Investment has been heavily subsidized through the availability of credit at low, or negative, real rates of interest. This has particularly been the case in those sectors favored by policymakers such as the so-called dynamic manufacturing industries. The result of the credit incentives has been twofold: (1) the more capital-intensive manufacturing sectors have grown the fastest, and (2) more capital-intensive technology has been selected in all sectors for the firms (projects) able to avail themselves of the subsidized credits. While promoting substantial industrial investment and growth, this policy has greatly exacerbated Brazil's labor absorption problem. It is interesting to speculate as to what type of industrial profile would have emerged in Brazil had labor use been subsidized instead of the use of capital.

The credit incentive schemes, financed through a multitude of different programs and institutions, have in large part bypassed SSE. This in fact can be considered a redeeming feature. Consequently, SSE has remained labor intensive, as was seen in table 3-5. The distortions visited upon the Brazilian industrial sector as a result of distortions imposed in factor markets through economic policy have left SSE largely untouched. Small enterprises have simply not been able to obtain large amounts of subsidized credits. Their partial exclusion from the official credit and banking system has made it impossible to reach SSE with subsidized credits in the absence of special programs designed to do so. And such programs have not existed in a meaningful way. Moreover, small firms have not been in a position to take advantage of exchange rate incentives to import capital equipment at overvalued exchange rates with tariff exemptions. Again, the effect has been largely beneficial in that it has prevented the growth and emergence of a capital-intensive SSE sector.

Despite the discriminatory dimensions in Brazilian economic policy designed to promote industrial development and the absence, at least until recently, of any special programs attendant to the needs of SSE, the small enterprise sector in Brazil is remarkably resilient and healthy. In fact, the failure of SSE to become more capital intensive like the rest of the industrial sector can be at least in part attributed to the fact that they have remained relatively untouched by government programs. The resilience of Brazilian SSE was demonstrated in table 3-5; the number of small enterprises grew substantially between 1950 and 1970, as did their employment and their value added. SSE is in no danger of disappearing in Brazil. This is not to say, however, that SSEs do not have serious problems or that special programs, designed to accentuate the special features of SSE, are not desirable.

The comparison of two industrial censuses for two different years as presented in table 3-5, while shedding light on the development of SSEs as a whole, does not permit the identification of what has happened to individual establishments over the period in question. For example, table 3-5 says nothing about the growth or disappearance of the individual small establishments existing in 1950. One can only surmise. The small establishments in 1970 might be different establishments altogether. Knowing something about the growth, survival, and mortality of individual SSEs, along with their causes, will permit the identification of problems facing SSE.

A recent study coordinated by Henrique Rattner at the Getulio Vargas Foundation's School of Business Administration in São Paulo has, for the first time in Brazil, addressed the problem of mortality and failure of small and medium sized industrial firms in Brazil through a longitudinal analysis.[13] Building upon a study done earlier which interviewed randomly selected small and medium-sized firms in 1963 and 1964, Rattner's team returned to the same firms in 1977 for a follow-up interview. These firms were spread across a number of manufacturing industries and were located in São Paulo, Salvador, or Porto Alegre. Out of the original 165 firms only

99 (60 percent) had survived until 1976. The mortality rate of 40 percent seems even higher in view of the sale of majority control of 16 of the surviving 99 firms to other individuals or firms. If this mortality experience for SME is representative, and there is no reason to believe that it is not, the relevant question concerns the factors associated with success or failure of individual firms.

Problems of Small and Medium-Sized Enterprise

The experience of growth, survival, and mortality for individual firms over time provides lessons as to the difficulties that small and medium-sized enterprises confront. In conjunction with information gained from other interviewing sources, the Rattner study provides a unique basis for drawing some conclusions as to the factors contributing to success or failure of SME.

After having eliminated some nineteen of the surviving firms which refused to be interviewed, the Rattner study undertook an analysis of the characteristics associated with survival. First, it was found that firm age is positively correlated with survival. Surviving firms tended to be relatively older than the group average. Mortality was particularly high for those firms which, at the time of the 1963 interview, had not yet attained three years of operation. Second, the individual firm's manufacturing sector was seen to be important. A firm had a greater probability of surviving if it was in an expanding industry, such as metal working or automobile parts. The highest rate of mortality was observed in the slow-growing textile industry. Thus, a growing market demand, perhaps consisting of an export market, as is most notable in the case of shoes, tends to be important as a factor contributing to the survival of small firms.

A third factor found to contribute to a firm's chances of survival is regional location. Of the three regions studied by Rattner, Salvador was found to have the highest SME mortality rate and Porto Alegre, the lowest. These differences have been attributed to regional differences in sectoral composition. Salvador, for example, had many textile firms, while São Paulo and Porto Alegre had more firms producing automobile parts, agricultural implements, and shoes. Another factor reflected in the observed regional firm mortality differences is what Rattner has termed a difference in "cultural background." The business ethics and determination of entrepreneurs descending from German and Italian immigrants, along with greater community stability in Porto Alegre and, to a lesser extent, São Paulo, were considered by Rattner to be important.

Summarizing the features found to be associated with survival in the Rattner study and examining their opposites to identify problems small firms face, a few implications are apparent. Small firms appear to have a reduced probability of surviving if they are: (1) young, especially less than three years old, (2) producing in an industry with a slowly growing demand, and (3) located in a region which is growing slowly.

Looking solely at the surviving firms in the Rattner study, a number of characteristics of the firms are noteworthy. First, many of the surviving firms have evidently been quite successful as witnessed by their growth in size. A full 83 percent of the responding firms indicated that they expanded their work force during the 1963-1976 period; over half of the firms had at least doubled their work force. A good number of firms grew to the extent that they no longer could be considered small firms. As seen in table 3-6, significant differences are seen in the comparison of the original 1963 sample with that of the reporting survivors. Seventeen firms (27 percent of the reporting survivors) by 1976 employed more than 200 employees. Small firms, if they can survive, frequently grow substantially.

A second noteworthy characteristic of the surviving firms in the Rattner study is the degree to which these firms have had export experience. A full 41 percent have exported, and 31 percent continue to export and view the export market as essential. This not only suggests that small firms are capable of exporting and successsfully competing in export markets but that export activity may be a key to success.

A third feature of the surviving firms concerns education. While the stereotype of small industrial entrepreneurs generally involves an individual without much formal education, this picture was not apparent in the case of the surviving firms in the Rattner study. Three-quarters, of the present entrepreneurs (managers) in the surviving firms had received some university-level instruction, and all had had at least some exposure to secondary school.[14] Moreover, there is an emphasis placed by the entreprenuers on the education of their own offspring. The dramatic expansion and

Table 3-6
Distribution, by Firm Size, of the Firms Observed in 1963 and 1977 in the Rattner Study
(percent)

Number of Employees	*1963*	*1977*
1-19	31.2	9.7
20-49	40.3	21.0
50-99	22.7	14.5
100-149	3.2	14.5
150-200	2.6	12.9
201 and above	—	27.4
Total	100.0	100.0

Source: Rattner et al., *Pequena e Média Empresa no Brasil: 1963-1976,* p. 76.

democraticization of the Brazilian university system in the past 15 years has meant that successful small businessmen almost always send their own sons to the university. The entrepreneurs themselves obviously consider education important, and part of their success as the managers of successful (that is, surviving) SSEs may stem from their own educational backgrounds.

Although analyzing the performance and characteristics of successful small firms illustrates some of the difficulties facing SSEs, a more direct approach is to examine the characteristics of failing firms and the apparent reasons for their failure. The Rattner study showed that the 40 percent of the original 165 firms that failed tended to be distinct from the total sample of SSEs in several ways. First, the failing firms tended to be quite small, with 50 percent having less than 20 employees. Second, contrary to the surviving firms, failing firms tended to be young, as noted. Over one-half of the failing firms were less than three years old in 1963. Finally, failing firms tend to be partnerships. Only 11 percent of the failed firms were single proprietorships.

The reasons given by the former entrepreneurs for the failure of their firms vary, but certain similarities are apparent. The most common reason given for the failure of the firm was competition. While this explanation can cover a large range of situations and more basic reasons, 39 percent of the failed firms indicated competition as the primary reason for their demise. In general, when the firm did not require more complex equipment and was using a relatively simple technology, the competition that was felt came from other small firms. Only in the case of sectors requiring sophisticated technology and equipment was the competition coming from large enterprises.

Financing is an important problem for SSEs. In the Rattner study the unavailability of credit, particularly for working capital, was cited by 25 percent of the failing firms as the principal reason for their failure. It is difficult for SSEs to obtain credit either from the private banking system or from official, government sources. While the public banking system now accounts for about 80 percent of all credit extended in Brazil, less than 40 percent of all the firms interviewed in the Rattner study had experience with government credit. For small firms in general this proportion is bound to be less, given the nature of the firms included in the Rattner study. There are definite problems of accessibility, and entrepreneurs complain bitterly about paperwork and bureaucratic requirements necessary in obtaining official credit. While only one-half of all the firms interviewed in the Rattner study admitted that they encounted problems in actually and finally obtaining credit, entrepreneurs thought that the lack of sufficient credit constituted a problem for SSE in general. Frequently, the complaint involved the magnitude of interest rates. Two-thirds of the failed firms thought that insufficient credit was the primary reason for small firm failure, although this explanation was not necessarily applicable in their case.

It has already been noted that a large proportion of the failed firms in the Rattner study were partnerships. It is not surprising to find that disagreements between partners over the period 1963-1976 constituted the third single most important reason for SSE failure given by the failing firms. Also related to this were other difficulties in providing continuity to the firm's operations over time. Since small firms are generally associated with a small number of key individuals, sickness and death were also contributing causes for failure. In the case of a small family firm, there is frequently no one available to take over for the principal owner and entrepreneur. Additional problems that SSEs encounter in Brazil, as seen from the Rattner study and elsewhere, include difficulties in obtaining skilled labor and in acquiring access to raw materials, particularly when the raw material supply is controlled by a large competitor.

Bearing in mind the varied problems of SSE, the question is what can be done in terms of policy to assist SSE. It is clear that little can be done about disagreements between partners, and that the problem of competition complained about by firms is frequently a disguise for a firm's management, production, and/or marketing difficulties. The major area where public policy can play an important role in ameliorating the problems facing SSE in Brazil is in the area of financing. The provision of credit is indeed the conventional policy handle on the problem, and the next section will examine the existing financing arrangements and programs available to small-scale enterprises.

Financing Small and Medium-Sized Industry

There are a number of credit programs in Brazil available to small and medium-sized industry. In examining these assorted programs individually, it will be argued that the total impact of these programs, while beneficial, is not sufficient to attend adequately to the varied credit needs and requirements of small enterprises in Brazil. The major credit programs to be discussed are: FINAME, PROGIRO, the POC program of the BNDE, the small and medium-sized industry financing program of the BNB, CEBRAE-assisted lending programs to micro enterprises through the state development banks, the Central Bank Resolution 388 program, Banco do Brasil programs, and regular commercial bank financing activities relevant to SSEs.[15]

A distinction should be made between those credit programs open to all firms and those especially designed for and restricted to small and medium-sized firms. The FINAME program (Special Agency for Industrial Financing) belongs to the first category. It includes, but it is not limited to, financing for small- and medium-scale industry (SMI). The FINAME is an affiliate of the National Development Bank (BNDE) and finances the purchase of machinery and equipment for industrial firms under very favorable, that is, subsidized, terms. In 1977 FINAME approved loans totaling Cr $27.2 billion (or U.S. $1.8 billion) of which Cr $2.6 billion (or 9.6 percent) was approved for small and medium-sized firms.[16] This proportion of FINAME lending, of course, is considerably beneath the share of SMI in total industrial value added. Moreover, it is likely that even this amount is concentrated among the larger firms within the BNDE classification for SMI.

The PROGIRO program is designed to attend to the working capital needs of SMI through a fund (in mid-1978) of approximately Cr $7 billion on the part of the Caixa Econômica Federal with on-lending through the state development and investment banks. Like other official credit programs, PROGIRO's interest rates are heavily subsidized. The nominal rates for small and medium firms are 22 and 27 percent annually. Inflation in 1977 was about 45 percent. The PROGIRO operational definitions for small and medium-sized industrial firms were annual sales of up to 35,000 MVRs (standard reference values) for small firms and up to 85,000 MVRs for medium-sized firms. In June 1978 these cutoff points were equal to Cr $40.8 million (U.S. $2.3 million) and Cr $97.8 million (U.S. $5.5 million), respectively. Both of these limits are substantial. A "small" firm under this definition, conservatively assuming an average fixed capital-output ratio of 1 and a capital-labor ratio of U.S. $10,000 per employee, could easily employ over 200 individuals. Thus, while ostensibly a program directed toward SMI, the PROGIRO program has the makings of a program which can conceivably leave truly small enterprises untouched. PROGIRO is still too new for an assessment of its performance, but previous experience with other programs suggest that upper limits on sales may very well define the composition of the firms making the greatest use of the funds in favor of larger firms.

While the National Development Bank (BNDE) has in general concentrated its efforts and resources on large industrial projects, there have been some concessions to the need to provide long-term financing to SMI. In 1965 the FIPEME fund was established within BNDE to finance fixed investment for the initiation or expansion of small and medium-sized industrial enterprises. Until the time of its replacement in 1974 by the POC (Programa de Operações Conjuntas) program, it had financed about 2,000 credit operations for SMI throughout Brazil, with the projects totaling U.S. $555 million (in 1973 prices and exchange rates).[17] This indicates that only about 1.4 percent of the SMI in the country were reached by the FIPEME program. Moreover, the average loan was much higher than would be supposed for an SSE lending program; the average FIPEME loan amounted to

U.S. $277,000. One study analyzing the FIPEME loans granted between January 1972 and July 1973 calculated that only 14 percent of the value of all FIPEME loans were made to firms employing less than 100 workers.[18] In view of the limited impact and the large size of loans, FIPEME cannot be thought of as having adequately attended to the credit needs of small-scale enterprises.

The establishment of the POC program by BNDE, replacing FIPEME, can be viewed in many ways as a continuation of FIPEME under another guise. To be sure, there were administrative changes and the use of POC resources was broadened to include working capital financing, as well as that for fixed assets. Yet, the guarantee requirements remained the same (real assets of 1.3 times the amount of the loan) and the firm size cutoff limits to qualify for credit have remained high. Under the POC operational definition a firm can be considered small or medium in size, and thus qualify for a loan, if its fixed assets plus the projected investment total less than 500,000 ORTNs (indexed treasury bonds). In June 1978 prices and exchange rates, this amounts to U.S. $7.5 million. Only the largest firms in the country cannot qualify for POCs subsidized credits.

The performance of POC and affiliated programs also suggests that small firms are not being reached. In 1977 BNDE programs, including POC and which involved financing through agents (APA), approved loans to 950 small and medium-sized firms, according to the BNDE definition based upon ORTNs. These loans totaled Cr $3.6 billion.[19] Accordingly, the average loan was Cr $3.8 million, or about U.S. $252,000—hardly a small loan. Of the total amount only about 17 percent went to firms whose fixed assets plus loan were equal to less than 50,000 ORTNs (about U.S. $750,000). Looking solely at the POC operations in national currency, 27 percent of the SMI loan total (Cr $1.9 billion) went to firms with fixed assets plus loans of less than 50,000 ORTNs. Even here, however, the average loan size was still rather high—about U.S. $100,000.

The oldest continuous official credit program exclusively for SMI is administered under the auspices of the Bank of the Northeast (BNB) with the cooperation of SUDENE. Loans for both fixed investment and working capital are provided. Established in 1967, the small and medium-sized industry financing program of the BNB through 1977 had financed 958 loans totaling Cr $1,248 million (in December 1977 prices).[20] The average loan thus amounted to Cr $1.3 million, or roughly U.S. $81,000. While the average loan is rather high for a program purporting to deal with SSE, it is nevertheless much lower than the comparable figures for BNDE-related programs.

Because of its lending at negative real rates of interest, and the resultant decapitalization, the BNB's resources for its SMI program have dwindled. Recent years have seen less activity than previously.[21] Furthermore, the average size of loan has increased. In the first two years the average loan size, in 1977 prices, was about one-half the average over the entire eleven-year period. This suggests that the program has been partially drawn away from its original purpose of extending loans to SSE.

One of the problems apparent in the BNB program, as is also the case in other official SSE lending programs, is a high degree of bureaucratization and, as a result, high administrative costs for the program. The loan application process is formidable and seems to restrict the access of smaller firms to credit. One participating development bank is reputed to require no less than forty-two documents and forms in support of a loan application. In the case of small firms possessing only rudimentary accounting practices, the requirements appear to be overly exacting. The accompanying delays are also substantial. Rarely is a loan actually dispersed within three months after application is undertaken. All of this, of course, results in substantial administrative costs. Streamlining the loan application process, perhaps with the use of credit-scoring techniques, would serve both to reduce administrative costs and to increase the accessibility of small firms to credit.

The size of the BNB SMI program must be considered quite small. As noted, only 958 loans have been approved in a period of eleven years. This represents only about 6 percent of the total eligible establishments in just Pernambuco, Bahia, and Ceará. If the BNB is to have a significant impact on SSE in the Northeast, its annual operations to SSE will have to be expanded substantially.

The SMI program of the BNB extends credit at negative real rates of interest. While it has been argued that such subsidies are politically (if not economically) necessary, the BNB, to its credit, has recently initiated a program with full monetary correction, instead of zero or partial monetary correction. This program, called the PCIS (Supplemental Industrial Credit Program), has grown and has enjoyed some success. Although not limited to SMI lending, some small and medium-sized firms have taken advantage of this line of credit.[22]

CEBRAE and its regional affiliates are often involved in the development of projects for financing by BNB. Technical assistance is frequently provided to obtain financing for SSE through credit institutions. In addition to the BNB program, CEBRAE affiliates are involved in a program to assist micro enterprises to obtain credit through the state development banks. Although the impact of this program has been positive, it appears rather modest in scope.

An attempt of the federal government to deal with the scarcity of working capital for SSEs is indicated in Resolution 338 of the Central Bank in 1976. According to this regulation, all commercial banks in Brazil are required to set aside an amount equal to 12 percent of their total demand deposits for lending to small and medium-sized enterprises. Accounts receivable are provided as guarantees for these loans for a period of twelve months. For the purposes of the program SME are defined as those firms with annual sales less than 85,000 times the standard reference value (that is, the MVR, which in June 1978 was equal to Cr $1,150.70). This means that firms can qualify if they have sales less than U.S. $5.5 million. As in the case of other programs designed to benefit SSEs, the cutoff limits for qualifying for the program are drawn very high so that firms that are indeed not small enterprises also qualify.

The interest rate for Resolution 388 borrowing is heavily subsidized—a mandated cost imposed by the Central Bank upon the commercial banks. As of mid-1978 Resolution 388 funds were being lent at a nominal interest rate of 16 percent. Naturally, at such an interest rate, given Brazilian conditions, there is a scramble for the available funds. The result is that very little of the mandated Resolution 388 resources end up being lent to SSEs. The original intention of Resolution 388 has been subverted. The commercial banks frequently use Resolution 388 lending as a bargaining instrument in their dealings with larger clients. Subsidized Resolution 388 funds are provided to the firm—or frequently to the economic group, of which the firm is a part—in return for the purchase of other types of banking services at non-subsidized prices. In the words of the president of one of the state development banks: "The resources of Resolution 388 are always lent to the SME which are the largest and/or are the best clients, and as such are capable of offering reciprocity to the banks."[23] The smallest firms, which are those generally most in need of credit, are left out. Especially if they are located in the lesser-developed areas of the country or outside the state capitals, they never even learn of the existence of the subsidized Resolution 388 or PROGIRO working capital credits.

The largest commercial bank in Brazil is the government-owned Banco do Brasil. In addition to its own Resolution 388 program, it also possesses, unlike most private banks, a number of special credit programs and lines. Except for one relatively modest program involving fixed-asset financing for SME, the Banco do Brasil's programs do not deal specifically with SME. As a whole, the Banco do Brasil has not directed large amounts of resources into SSE.

For their part, the commercial banks have also neglected the SSEs and their special credit problems and need. The transaction costs of lending to SSEs, or in making small loans in general, are higher than for other types of lending. To the extent that commercial banks do lend to SSE these higher transaction costs, as well as a premium for perceived higher risk, are recouped in higher interest rates. A problem is that commercial banks frequently do not want to be bothered with SSE, and they simply are not equipped to deal with SSE. The lending to SSE that does take place by commercial banks is short-term in nature and commonly involves the discounting of accounts receivable.

As indicated in table 3-7, private interest rate charges in Brazil during 1978 were high, even discounting the inflation. Compensating balances are required by commercial banks, rendering the effective charges high in nominal terms, and, in some cases, even high in real terms. Small firms, to the extent that they can obtain credit at all, are generally forced to pay the highest effective interest rates. There is a demand, however, for credit at positive real interest rates, and SSEs are frequently willing and able to pay these rates.

This situation, depicted in table 3-7 for 1978, has become exacerbated since then. As inflation accelerated in the second half of 1979, the government undertook measures to control interest rates. With the arbitrary fixing of monetary correction at 45 percent in January 1980 for all of 1980, all government-controlled interest rates became negative, and substantially so, in real terms. In addition to creating adverse distortions, discouraging savings, and misallocating economic resources on the whole, the increasing financial repression, as witnessed during the first half of 1980, can be expected to result in nonmarket credit rationing on the part of financial institutions. As is generally the case, the major victims of such financial repression are small enterprises. These firms find themselves increasingly cut off from the organized, and repressed, credit markets and at a considerable disadvantage.

Summary and Concluding Remarks

The current state of repressed financial markets is consistent with the historical development of SSE in Brazil. The small-scale industrial sector has been largely bypassed in the process of Brazilian industrialization. Economic policies to promote industrial development have in effect concen-

Table 3-7
The Annual Nominal Cost of Short-Term Borrowing from Brazilian Commercial Banks, May 1978
(percent)

Category	*Monthly Interest and Charges*	*Required Compensating Balance*	*Effective Annual Cost of Borrowing*
Cheap	2.1	10.0	33.2
Average	2.4	30.0	53.1
Expensive	2.5	35.0	61.7
Very Expensive	4.2	33.3	124.4

Source: "Quem Lucra com o Dineiro Caro," *Visão,* May 1, 1978, p. 51. The information was compiled from an interviewing survey of eleven commercial banks.

trated on bigness. Government enterprises and transnational corporations, both of which are relatively large in scale, have played important roles in Brazil's substantial industrial growth during the past 25 years. Despite the impressive gains made by large-scale firms, SSEs continue to be important in the economy. They are significant in providing employment, making the economy more responsive to change, and serving as a training ground for entrepreneurs.

This analysis of the participation of SSE in the Brazilian manufacturing sector has been undertaken with data from the 1970 industrial census. Previous analysis has frequently been based upon less comprehensive IBGE annual industrial survey information. The data employed in the study are the best available in Brazil to date for analyzing SSE. Importantly, unlike the incomparable annual IBGE surveys, the 1970 census information lends itself to comparison with previous censuses.

When comparing SSE with larger enterprises in Brazil two characteristics stand out. First, average wages are less in small enterprises, indicating a less intensive use of skilled labor. Second, the capital intensity of SSE is lower than that for larger manufacturing establishments. Value added per worker in general increases with the size of establishment. On the basis of some production function analysis for SSE and the examination of some existing SME lending programs in Brazil, some estimates of the capital cost per job were developed. Our best aggregative estimate is that it costs about U.S. $4,000 to create a job in Brazilian SSE.

To analyze the aggregate performance of SSE over time a comparison of the 1950 and 1970 industrial censuses was made. The results demonstrate that SSE in Brazil has grown. Despite severe problems and difficulties SSE shows a certain amount of resilience and vitality. In relative terms, between 1950 and 1970 its share in the total number of establishments and total manufacturing employment has remained virtually unchanged. The SSE share of manufacturing value added, however, has fallen. While medium and large scale establishments recorded significant increases in value added per worker, SSEs witnessed little in the way of increases in labor productivity. Small-scale industry in Brazil has remained relatively labor intensive. It is argued that in great part the reasons for this differing performance between SSEs and larger establishments relate to the impact of economic policy. Through a myriad of programs and incentives industrial policy has had an effect of increasing the capital intensity of the Brazilian industrial economy, while leaving SSEs largely untouched.

If the results of the only longitudinal study of Brazilian SME are at all representative, the mortality rate for SME in Brazil is rather high. Over a thirteen year period a mortality rate for established firms of 40 percent was observed. The reasons for failure underline the problems that small and medium sized firms confront in Brazil. A major difficulty that can be meaningfully addressed by government policy is the perceived scarcity of credit available to SSE.

The existing financing programs and institutional arrangements in Brazil largely bypass SSE. The private banking sector, accounting for only about 20 percent of all loans extended in the country, has generally, and with some reason, been unresponsive to the credit needs and requirements of SSE. The official programs, of which there are several, also are not sufficient to attend adequately to the special and varied credit problems of small enterprises in Brazil. The resources of these programs are not particularly large, but, more importantly, there is a tendency to concentrate banking efforts on the larger firms within the range of those that qualify. These firms are almost never small-scale enterprises.

To the extent that subsidized credit in Brazil has contributed to the growth in the capital intensity of the larger manufacturing enterprises, the failure to reach SSE with subsidized credit can be thought of in more positive terms. Indeed, a compelling argument can be made, for the economy as a whole, for nonrepressed financial markets, implying, of course, positive real interest rates. As far as SSEs are concerned, efforts to provide financing to such firms should clearly involve lending at positive real rates of interest. Otherwise, the increase in SSE financing will result in an erosion of the attraction of the small-scale industrial sector as a provider of employment in a surplus labor economy.

Notes

1. See, for example, Joel Bergsman, *Brazil: Industrialization and Trade Policies* (London: Oxford University Press, 1970) and Werner Baer, *Industrialization and Economic Development in Brazil* (Homewood, Illinois: Richard D. Irwin, 1965).

2. In June 1978 the cruzeiro-dollar exchange rate was Cr $17.60 = U.S. $1.00.

3. A later industrial census was conducted for 1975. As of July 1980, the results were not yet available. It is doubtful, however, that there has been observed much change in the relative importance of SME. Using the 1970 IBGE industrial census data provides another important advantage. The published census data, because of some omissions and incomparabilities, is not particularly suitable for the type of analysis depicted in table 3-1. CEBRAE, however, has had IBGE undertake some special computations from the census tapes. CEBRAE has been kind enough to make these special tabulations available; and it is these data that have been employed in our analysis.

4. An alternative definitional treatment, involving the use of sales in-

formation as the discriminating criterion, has been used to develop appendix table C-1. The most comprehensive and best analysis available of SME in Brazil is Frederico Robalinho de Barros and Rui Lyrio Modenesi, *Pequenas a Médias Indústrias: Análise dos Problemas, Incentivos a sua Contribuição ao Desenvolvimento*, Relatório de Pesquisa No. 17 (Rio De Janeiro: IPEA/INPES, 1973). Unfortunately, Robalinho and Modenesi did not have the results of the 1970 industrial census available at the time of writing. Instead, they relied upon a less complete IBGE industrial survey for 1969. Because of sampling procedure changes, intertemporal comparisons of the IBGE annual industrial surveys are highly misleading.

5. See appendix table C-2.

6. See, World Bank, *Employment and Development of Small Enterprises: A Sector Policy Paper*, prepared by the Industrial Development and Finance Department (Washington: World Bank, February 1978).

7. The use of value added per employee as a proxy for capital intensity (that is, the K/L ratio) necessarily implies that there are no systematic differences in the average productivity of capital over firms. This can be seen in the tautology $VA/L = VA/K \cdot K/L$. If more capital-intensive firms systematically exhibited lower average capital productivity (that is, lower VA/K), it is possible that there is no difference in the VA/L ratio. In our case we have no reason to believe that small establishments demonstrated appreciably *lower* average productivities for capital.

8. A more general functional form could be employed at the cost of some simplicity and additional necessary assumptions. The Cobb-Douglas functional form, however, does not appear to be unduly unreasonable, given a growing body of supporting empirical evidence.

9. NAE/CE, "Programa de Financiamento da Pequena e Média Indústria," report of the Banco de Nordeste do Brasil e Centro de Apoio à Pequena e Média Empresa de Estado de Ceará, May 1978, p. 11.

10. It should be noted that medium-sized establishments have been defined in table 3-5 to encompass larger firms than before, that is, those establishments having between 100 and 499 persons employed.

11. See Regis Bonelli, *Tecnologia e Crescimento Industrial: A Experiencia Brasileira nos Anos 60*, IPEA/INPES Monografia No. 25 (Rio de Janeiro: IPEA/INPES, 1976).

12. See Eugene Staley and Richard Morse, *Modern Small Industry for Developing Countries*, (New York: McGraw Hill, 1965).

13. Henrique Rattner et al. *Pequena e Média Empresa no Brasil: 1963-1976*, unpublished book manuscript, São Paulo, May 1978.

14. Ibid, p. 149. The unusually high educational attainment reported in the surviving firms is not representative of SSE management in general. The selected firms were all located in capital cities where educational levels and opportunities have always been higher, especially in Porto Alegre and São

Paulo. Furthermore, it has been noted that the firms in question are the *surviving* firms, frequently operating in industries in which some technical knowledge is essential. Also, a selectivity bias may be evident in the exclusion of those successful firms which refused to be interviewed. Since by their refusal the managers of these firms have shown themselves less interested in research and university contacts, they are probably less likely to have been exposed to a university environment.

15. A list of abbreviations and acronyms follows the preface.

16. BNDE, *Relatório de Atividades*, 1977, p. 32.

17. Frederico Robalinho de Barros, "O Problema do Financiamento à Pequena e Média Indústria no País," unpublished IPEA/INPES report, December 1974. Robalinho concludes that "the truly small and medium sized industrial firms in the country were not benefitted by FIPEME, but were instead marginalized from the financing process." p. 6.

18. Francisco E. Thoumi, "A Report on the Size Structure of Industry in Brazil with Special Reference to Small-Scale Industry," unpublished paper, IBRD, November 3, 1973.

19. BNDE, *Relatório Anual de Atividades, 1977*, Area de Projetos com Agentes, ASCOA/APA.

20. BNB, "Programa de Financiamento da Pequena e Média Indústria," unpublished report, May 1978.

21. The program's real lending total for 1977 was smaller than that for either of the first full two years of the program.

22. In 1977 loans authorized under PCIS totaled Cr $205 million, of which less than 10 percent went to SME. BNB, *Relatório, 1977*, p. 44.

23. Quoted from a speech manuscript in preparation.

Appendix 3A: Estimations for Fixed Capital Costs per Job for Brazilian Small-Scale Industry

Begin by assuming the constant-returns-to-scale form of the Cobb-Douglas production function for all small-scale industrial firms in Brazil:

$$X_i = A\, K_i^{\alpha} L_i^{\beta}, \qquad \alpha + \beta = 1 \tag{3.1}$$

where

X_i = firm's i's output, or value added, measured in money terms
K_i = firm i's fixed capital assets, measured in money terms
L_i = the labor employed in firm i, measured in man-years
A = a technological constant
α,β = the output elasticities with respect to capital and labor. Differentiating 3.1 to obtain the marginal products of capital K and labor L, and assuming that the price-taking small firms are successful in maximizing profits so as to equate the marginal productivities with factor prices, a well-known property of the Cobb-Douglas production function is obtained:

$$\frac{rK}{wL} = \frac{\alpha}{\beta} \tag{3.2}$$

where r and w are the costs of capital and labor, respectively. Thus, the ratio of the factor income shares is equal to the ratio of their output elasticities. Manipulating 3.2 we have:

$$K/L = \frac{\alpha/\beta}{r/w} = \alpha/\beta \bullet w/r$$

Therefore, knowing, or assuming, factor prices and the values of the parameters α and β, the capital cost per job is determinate.

Values of $\alpha = 0.20$ and $\beta = 0.80$ have been assumed. That these are reasonable values is suggested by a study undertaking such estimates for SEE in Colombia.[1]

Two estimates of the wage rate were utilized, as seen in table 3A-1. The first, Cr \$20,280, is an annualized current minimum wage. The second wage estimate, Cr \$26,205, is equal to the ratio of the observed average wages for small establishments in 1970 to the prevailing annualized minimum wage in

1970 multiplied by the 1978 annualized minimum wage. Various assumptions concerning the real cost of capital (interest rate *r*) are given in table 3A-1.

Table 3A-1
Estimates of Fixed Investment per Worker Using a Cobb-Douglas Production Function for Small Enterprises
(U.S. dollars)

Annual Average Wage (W) (1978 Prices)	*Interest Rate (r)*				
	.06	*.08*	*.10*	*.12*	*.15*
Cr $20,280	4,592	3,444	2,755	2,296	1,837
Cr $26,205	5,934	4,451	3,560	2,967	2,374

Note

1. See William G. Tyler and Lung-Fei Lee, "On Estimating Stochastic Frontier Production Functions and Average Efficiency: An Empirical Analysis with Colombian Micro Data," *The Review of Economics and Statistics,* 51, no. 3 (August 1979).

4 Technical Efficiency in the Industrial Sector

Introduction

In recent years there has been an increase in interest on the part of economists in the problem of measuring technical efficiency. The exercise of managerial abilities to use productive factors in the most technically efficient manner is a matter of concern for both economic theorists and policymakers. Much of the recent literature has focused on the concept of the production frontier as a tool for measuring and analyzing efficiency. With such an approach much of the empirical work has involved estimation with aggregate data (Farrell 1957; Timmer 1971; Aigner, Lovell, and Schmidt 1977). While estimation with micro data seems superior, such empirical work either does not involve firm-specific measures of technical efficiency (Richmond 1974; Meeusen and van den Broeck 1977; Lee and Tyler 1978) or, if firm-specific measures are developed, the estimation of the production frontier is undertaken with nonstochastic procedures (Meller 1976; Tyler 1979). In the latter case, observational outliers resulting from measurement error can seriously affect the results.

To overcome the problem of estimating sensitivity to measurement error while, at the same time, permitting the development of firm-specific measures of relative technical efficiency, this chapter employs an alternative to the production frontier approach. Instead, an average production function is estimated by ordinary least-squares methods, where firm-specific intercepts, representing individual firm efficiency relative to the average production function, are also estimated. This procedure is stochastic in nature and in essence amounts to an analysis of covariance. It has been employed by Hoch (1955), Mundlak (1961), and Gunter and Emerson (1977) to deal with the problem of management bias in production function estimation. A pooling of firm cross-section and time-series data is undertaken. The departure of our analysis is a more specific specification of technological change and an application to both industrial firm data and data from a developing country. The Brazilian manufacturing sector has grown dramatically and is thought to be in some ways representative of rapidly growing, dynamic manufacturing sectors in other developing countries.

There is some evidence to suggest that there exists substantial technical inefficiency in industrial production in Brazil. Stories and anecdotes abound concerning incidents and situations reflecting X-inefficiency on the part of the individual firms. These stories, indicating that there is considerable variation in managerial efficiency, are consistent with the fact that the Brazilian manufacturing sector is heavily protected from import competition. By permitting domestic manufacturing prices to be consistently higher than international prices, the protection system, along with the absence of rigorous domestic market price competition, allows a quiet, profitable life for many manufacturing establishments. Highly inefficient firms seem to be able to survive alongside extremely efficient firms.

Some econometric evidence of the wide variation in technical efficiency across firms has been provided by recent attempts to estimate frontier production functions with Brazilian data. One such study (Lee and Tyler 1978), employing 1971 data from some 850 manufacturing firms, estimated that the average level of actual output realized by firms was only 63-70 percent of the possible output, measured as production on the estimated stochastic production function frontier. More disaggregated analysis for the steel and plastics industries (Tyler 1979), while estimating the production frontier by nonstochastic procedures, provided similar evidence of widespread technical inefficiency. The implication of this analysis, along with the anecdotal materials concerning X-inefficiency in Brazilian manufacturing establishments, is that substantial one-shot increases in industrial output could be obtained through the reduction of technical inefficiency.

The use of the analysis of covariance procedure permits the development of a measure of relative technical efficiency. There is an important difference between such a measure, however, and an efficiency measure derived from an estimated production frontier. With the latter approach a cardinal measure of technical efficiency is possible, in relation to the frontier. This efficiency index is the ratio of observed output, given its factor usage, to potential output on the production frontier. Such an index is not possible, however, with the use of the analysis of covariance procedure. With this procedure technical efficiency is seen as relative to an average production function rather than a frontier production function. As such, the cardinality of the efficiency measure possesses less economic meaning. Nevertheless, in addition to the ordinality of the measure being still valid, the cardinal differences in efficiency between firms are still meaningful, but as related to mean efficiency rather than to the best-use practice. This does not constitute a drawback, however, as it is the analysis of relative efficiency over firms which is of importance and interest.

The question of the relative efficiency of foreign versus domestically owned firms is one which has received much polemical, although little analytical, attention. On one hand, the defenders of the interests of the multinational firms allege that those firms are more efficient and provide functioning mechanisms for significant technological transfer. In fact, it is their greater relative technical efficiency which is frequently used to justify multinational firm operations in developing countries. On the other end of the political spectrum, those individuals attacking the multinational firms as essentially exploitative institutions rarely question the greater technical efficiency of foreign firms operating in developing countries. On the contrary, it is argued that it is the technological superiority of the multinationals which imperils national enterprise. To be sure, if in fact multinationals are more efficient than domestically owned firms, the implications for future growth, dependence, and possible denationalization of the domestic economy are great. The question then rests on whether indeed there is evidence to support the allegation that foreign firms are more efficient than domestically owned firms. Our firm-specific technical efficiency estimates permit some exploratory analysis of this question. In addition, the relationship between efficiency, on one hand, and profitability and firm size, on the other, can also be examined.

The following section develops the analytical framework and discusses the estimating procedures employed. Subsequent sections contain a description of the data; presentation of the empirical results; the results of the exploratory, bivariate analysis of the relationship between efficiency, ownership, profitability, and firm size; and some concluding remarks.

Analytical Framework and Measurement Techniques

The exercise of managerial abilities and technological know-how are obviously important components in the production process. Since they are not directly observable, they are subsumed in the intercept of the production function. Yet, it is likely that there will be a positive relationship between technical efficiency and factor usage. Well-managed and efficient firms presumably will be successful, and will use more productive factors than less-efficient firms. If this is indeed the case, a management bias is likely to be evident in empirical estimates of production functions.

Consider as an illustration figure 4-1. With the indicated observation points a log-linear ordinary least-squares (OLS) estimation of the production function would estimate the regression plane *AB*. Now assume that the observed-firm observation points belong to two separate groups of firms: efficient large firms and inefficient small firms. The "true" average production functions for efficient and inefficient firms are f_1 and f_2, respectively. As such, the slope of the regression plane *AB* overstates the output elasticities. In other words, the output elasticities are biased upward because of the management bias. Assuming no differences in output elasticities between efficient and inefficient firms, the management bias can be removed by estimating the separate intercepts *D* and *C*.

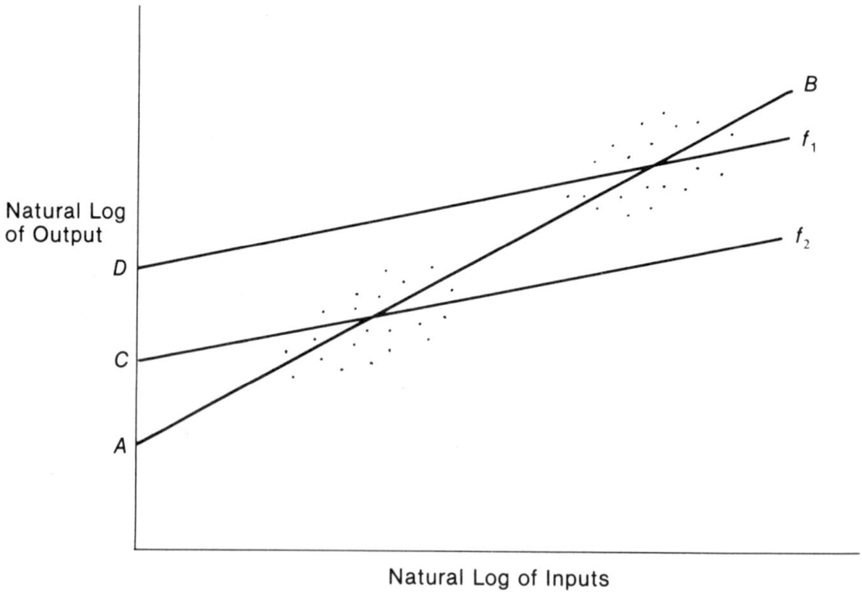

Figure 4-1. Management Bias in Production Function Estimation

Consider the Cobb-Douglas production function

$$X_{ij} = AK_{ij}^{\alpha}L_{ij}^{\beta} \tag{4.1}$$

where

X_{ij} = output for the ith firm in period j
A = a technological constant, representative of technical efficiency
K_{ij} = capital stock for i^{th} firm in period j
L_{ij} = labor employed in the ith firm in period j

Equation 4.1 is log-linear and can be estimated in single equation form by OLS as

$$x_{ij} = a + \alpha k_{ij} + \beta 1_{ij} + u_{ij} \tag{4.2}$$

where the lower cases of the variables represent the natural logarithms and where u represents an error term, about which the standard assumptions are made. The estimation of 4.2 assumes that A is both time- and firm-invariant, and that α and β also do not differ over time or firms. As indicated, all managerial and technological considerations are subsumed in A, and the estimation of 4.2 will possess managerial bias.

To incorporate the possibility of firm-variant and time-variant intercepts we can rewrite equation 4.1 as:

$$X_{ij} = A_o A_i A_j K_{ij}^{\alpha} L_{ij}^{\beta}, \tag{4.3}$$

where A_i and A_j depict multiplicative increments (reductions) in the average intercept for individual firms and time periods. Such a specification has a log-linear counterpart similar to equation 4.2 and is

$$x_{ij} = a_o + a_i + a_j + \alpha k_{ij} + \beta 1_{ij} + u_{ij}. \tag{4.4}$$

Following Mundlak (1976), the term a_i, depicting the individual firm's intercept relative to the average production function, can be viewed alternatively as equal to cm_i, where m_i is the unobserved management input, in logs, for firm i, and where c represents the constant output elasticity for that management input, that is,

$$a_i = cm_i. \tag{4.5}$$

Normalizing a_i such that $\Sigma_i a_i = 0$, estimates of a_o, α, β, and a_i can be obtained by OLS. The variable a_i is a firm-specific dummy variable for each individual firm. The assumption is made that a_o, c, α, and β for the cross-section are unchanged over time.[1]

The assumption that α and β remain constant over time does not preclude shifts in the production function due to technological progress. Unlike the estimates undertaken by Hoch and Mundlak with firm data, production function estimates with micro data for industrial firms are not subject to year-to-year fluctuations in weather. Consequently, shifts in the production function can be considered to reflect more accurately technological change. The multiplicative time intercept A_j could be depicted as a time-specific dummy variable. Instead, however, we have specified a continuous rate of Hicksian neutral technological progress, such that

$$X_{ij} = A_o e^{\lambda t} A_i K_{ij}^{\alpha} L_{ij}^{\beta} \tag{4.6}$$

and

$$x_{ij} = a_o + \lambda t + a_i + \alpha k_{ij} + \beta 1_{ij} + u_{ij}, \tag{4.7}$$

where t equals discrete time in annual intervals and λ can be interpreted as the annual proportional rate of technical progress.

There is still no estimate of c—the output elasticity with respect to the unobservable management input m_i. By imposing the admittedly restrictive condition that the production function exhibits constant returns to scale we have

$$c = 1 - (\hat{\alpha} + \hat{\beta}). \tag{4.8}$$

Since α and β, as estimated in equation 4.7 are unbiased estimates, c represents an unbiased estimate of the output elasticity for management.

From the estimates obtained through the fitting of equation 4.7 we can derive a firm-specific index measuring the firm's technical efficiency relative to the average. Incorporating the shifts due to technical progress, it is written as

$$E_i = \frac{A_o A_i}{A_o}. \tag{4.9}$$

In the empirical analysis that follows, this index is computed for each firm for which the OLS regression coefficient for the firm dummy variable a_i was statistically significant at the 5 percent level.

The Data

The data employed for the empirical estimates are data for individual firms in selected Brazilian manufacturing industries covering the years 1971-1975. The data were compiled on an annual basis from balance sheet information made available in the *Visão* series.[2] For the most part, information was available at the two- or three-digit level. The data did not permit further disaggregation. The number of firms in each industry, of course, varied but generally exceeded twenty, although in some cases data for each firm were not available for all of the five years.[3] While the coverage of firms in the survey is not complete, the major firms in the selected industries are included. The firms omitted from the survey are the smallest firms, and as a result there are very few firms included in the sample having less than 200 employees.

The noninclusion of the smallest firms can be seen as an advantage for two reasons. First, since smaller firms frequently produce altogether different products in any industry grouping, their noninclusion diminishes the problem of product heterogeneity. Second, by concentrating on the large and medium-sized firms the dichotomy of traditional versus modern, present in a dual economy such as Brazil, is reduced. Our analysis deals with the relatively "modern" firms.

Data compiled from the corporate reports and balance sheets included information on net assets, fixed capital assets, profits, employees, and sales. Subsequently, the firms were identified by ownership, with over 50 percent of ownership determining whether the firm was classified as foreign, private domestic, or government.[4] In the analysis presented here there were very few government firms included in the sample.

The capital variable used in the production function estimates is a stock variable representing the annual current price value of the firm's total fixed physical capital. Although expressed in money terms, the values are adjusted to the prices of the year in question via the application of the so-called "monetary correction" coefficients as stipulated in Brazilian tax law. With Brazil's rapid rate of inflation, a historical book-value measure of the capital stock would be meaningless. During the 1971-1975 period the monetary correction system worked reasonably well, with the coefficients accurately reflecting the rates of inflation. Our capital measure ideally should represent the capital stock's market value in current prices for the years in question. It probably does not do so entirely because of accelerated depreciation schemes, which have the effect of understating the actual capital stock.[5]

Labor services in the production function are measured in units of total employee man-years. While it may be preferable to consider only production employees, this information was not available. Our procedure is rationalized on the grounds that a modern firm necessarily requires non-production workers in its operations, and the measure of the firm's efficiency must relate to the way in which those workers are related to sales and output.

The major measurement problem deals with the measure of output. Regrettably, value added information was not available from the balance sheet information making up the data file; it was necessary to use current-price sales data as a proxy for firm output. Since inventories were not seen to fluctuate greatly, sales constitute a reasonable measure of total firm output. Yet, because of the failure to consider intermediate inputs, there is a problem of an omitted variable when analyzing production behavior. The use of value added data, if available, would preclude this difficulty. Instead, we are forced to assume implicitly that the ratio of value added to total output is a random variable over the firm population.[6] If it is not, differences in measured inefficiency may simply reflect differences in the extent to which manufacturing processes are vertically integrated within firms.

Since the annual data for sales, fixed capital assets, net assets, and profits are all in current prices for the year in question, price adjustments were necessary. The deflators used were the standard price indices computed by the Getulio Vargas Foundation and published in *Conjuntura Econômica*. Sales were deflated by the wholesale industrial price indexes for the relevant product groups. The other current price variables were deflated by the wholesale industrial price index. All deflated variables were expressed in 1971 prices in thousands of cruzeiros (Cr $1000).

Empirical Analysis and Results

The first test performed with the data dealt with the question of the appropriateness of data pooling. An *F*-test was undertaken to test the null hypothesis of equality of the parameters for the different Cobb-Douglas production functions estimated over different annual interfirm cross-sections. In all of the industries with results reported in this study the null hypothesis could not be rejected at the one percent level of confidence. Therefore, pooling of the time-series information for firms with the interfirm cross-section was undertaken.

The results of the production function estimates with the pooled data are presented in table 4-1 for the industries in question. For comparison purposes, equations (a) and (b) in that table do not include the individual firm intercepts. A test for constant returns to scale, that is, $\alpha + \beta = 1$, was undertaken. For nine of the fourteen included industries the null of constant returns to scale could not be rejected.[7] For the remaining five industries it was rejected. Decreasing returns to scale were observed in the electrical equipment, chemical, and petroleum industries, while evidence of increasing returns was found in the perfumery and plastics industries (table 4-1).

Some indirect tests as to the appropriateness of the Cobb-Douglas functional form were also undertaken. Following procedures employed by Griliches and Ringstad (1971), single equation estimates of the Kmenta approximation for the OLS production function and of a translog production function were carried out. In all cases the Cobb-Douglas functional form could not be rejected.[8]

The results of estimating the basic Cobb-Douglas function in equation 4.2, and its extension to include Hicks neutral technological progress, are presented as equations (a) and (b) in table 4-1 for the industries in question. As is seen, the fits are generally good, with output elasticities taking on reasonable values. In most cases the regression coefficients are significant at the 5 percent level. The results of the covariance model estimates of the production function, incorporating the individual firm intercepts, appear as equations (c) and (d) in table 4-1, corresponding respectively to equations 4.4 and 4.7. With the individual firm intercepts, removing managerial bias from the production function estimates generally brings about substantial reductions in the output elasticities for capital and labor.

On the assumption that the production functions exhibit constant returns to scale with Hicks neutral technological progress, the output elasticity with respect to management, that is, c, can be estimated. For the industries for which the constant-returns-to-scale hypothesis could not be rejected and for which the regression coefficients in equation (d) were significant at the 5 percent level, the estimates of c are reported in table 4-1. These estimates of managerial output elasticity range from 0.11 (apparel) to 0.58 (textile spinning and weaving). Management and managerial capabilities seem to be important inputs in the production process for the included industries.

In all specifications estimated the selected industries are seen to demonstrate relatively high rates of technological progress. With the covariance model estimates, the observed annual rates of Hicks neutral technological change for the 1971-1975 period were estimated. The period was one of dramatic industrial growth in Brazil, and our selected industries include some of the most rapidly growing (for example, machinery, chemicals) as well as some of slower growing industries (textile, apparel). In all industries but one (perfumery and cosmetic products) the estimated rates of Hicks neutral technological progress were statistically significant at the 5 percent level. In all cases technological progress was seen to be an important component accounting for Brazilian growth. The rates, expressed annually, ranged from a low 4.8 percent for plastics to a high of 23.6 percent for office machinery. The magnitude of these rates, indicating the importance of technological change, suggests the need for further, more detailed, and more solidly based research on the nature and characteristics of technological progress in Brazilian industry.

Employing the estimates of a_i from the estimates of equation 4.7, the technical efficiency index $E_i = A_iA_0/A_0$ was constructed for each firm in each of the industries in question. For these computations the assumption of constant returns to scale is no longer necessary, as it was in the estimation of the output elasticity with respect to managerial inputs c. Individual firm efficiency varies relative to the average practice as indicated by the estimated production function. However, in our estimations the individual firm intercepts a_i's were not always significant. Therefore, only in the case of statistical significance at the 5 percent level was the computed, firm-specific technical efficiency index actually employed in the subsequent analysis of the relationships between technical efficiency and other economic variables. This procedure accordingly reduced the possible set of firms in each industry.

Table 4-1
Cobb-Douglas Production-Function Estimates for Selected Brazilian Manufacturing Industries, Pooled Time Series and Interfirm Cross-Sectional Data

Industry		*Number of Observations* (N)	*Intercept ln A*	α	β	γ	*Inclusion of Firm Intercepts* a_i	$\bar{R}^2$	*SEE*	*Returns to Scale and Estimates of c in the case of Constant Returns to Scale (CRS)*[c]
Equipment and motor machinery										
	(a)	602	4.533	0.332[a] (6.826)[b]	0.611 (17.902)	—	no	0.63	0.572	—
	(b)	602	3.995	0.333 (7.321)	0.630 (19.643)	0.156 (9.128)	no	0.68	0.536	—
	(c)	602	5.284	0.207 (5.137)	0.503 (12.758)	—	yes	0.70	0.519	—
	(d)	602	5.291	0.158 (4.354)	0.479 (13.496)	0.178 (11.068)	yes	0.76	0.465	0.36
Office machinery										
	(a)	48	4.191	0.134 (1.434)	0.819 (7.748)	—	no	0.67	0.613	—
	(b)	48	3.454	0.141 (1.609)	0.853 (8.560)	0.177 (2.726)	no	0.71	0.573	—
	(c)	48	4.427	0.436 (2.826)	0.366 (2.537)	—	yes	0.81	0.465	—
	(d)	48	4.183	0.310 (2.767)	0.408 (3.970)	0.236 (5.604)	yes	0.90	0.330	0.28

Electrical equipment									
(a)	160	4.382	0.334 (4.951)	0.591 (6.854)	—	no	0.52	0.668	—
(b)	160	4.132	0.320 (4.899)	0.524 (7.162)	0.131 (3.470)	no	0.55	0.648	—
(c)	160	5.869	0.128 (1.506)	0.548 (4.702)	—	yes	0.79	0.439	—
(d)	160	6.658	0.028 (3.29)	0.440 (4.485)	0.178 (6.979)	yes	0.86	0.364	DRS
Domestic appliances and communications equipment									
(a)	160	3.665	0.196 (2.583)	0.809 (10.528)	—	no	0.77	0.634	—
(b)	160	3.181	0.206 (2.857)	0.811 (11.101)	0.148 (4.184)	no	0.79	0.603	—
(c)	160	4.447	0.257 (2.819)	0.611 (6.221)	—	yes	0.91	0.397	—
(d)	160	5.489	0.174 (2.326)	0.421 (5.048)	0.177 (7.718)	yes	0.94	0.322	0.41
Chemicals and chemical products									
(a)	529	5.188	0.221 (6.392)	0.571 (12.885)	—	no	0.50	0.918	—
(b)	529	4.944	0.215 (6.247)	0.586 (13.204)	0.084 (2.742)	no	0.50	0.912	—
(c)	529	7.440	0.059 (1.510)	0.347 (6.933)	—	yes	0.68	0.734	—
(d)	529	7.236	0.040 (1.049)	0.360 (7.326)	0.110 (4.364)	yes	0.69	0.719	DRS

Table 4-1 *(continued)*

Industry	*Number of Observations* (N)	*Intercept ln A*	α	β	γ	*Inclusion of Firm Intercepts* a_i	$\bar{R}^2$	*SEE*	*Returns to Scale and Estimates of c in the case of Constant Returns to Scale (CRS)*[c]
Petroleum Refining									
(a)	95	4.201	0.651 (7.847)	0.273 (2.681)	—	no	0.87	0.698	—
(b)	95	3.995	0.663 (8.065)	0.255 (2.522)	0.097 (1.830)	no	0.87	0.689	—
(c)	95	6.743	0.533 (4.497)	−0.458 (1.680)	—	yes	0.96	0.399	—
(d)	95	8.879	0.366 (3.543)	−0.734 (1.866)	0.166 (5.528)	yes	0.97	0.332	DRS
Pharmaceutical products									
(a)	139	5.518	−0.079 (0.611)	0.929 (6.331)	—	no	0.31	1.079	—
(b)	139	4.837	−0.062 (0.490)	0.936 (6.508)	0.182 (2.570)	no	0.34	1.058	—
(c)	139	3.349	0.176 (0.687)	0.988 (4.194)	—	yes	0.40	1.008	—
(d)	139	3.087	0.219 (.878)	0.855 (3.647)	0.190 (2.616)	yes	0.44	0.900	n.s.
Perfumery and cosmetic products									
(a)	53	−0.072	0.909 (16.245)	0.454 (4.325)	—	no	0.86	0.731	—
(b)	53	−0.261	0.905 (15.886)	0.472 (4.257)	0.042 (0.547)	no	0.85	0.737	—
(c)	53	0.350	1.010 (29.410)	0.198 (1.779)	—	yes	0.96	0.408	—
(d)	53	0.130	1.006 (29.591)	0.206 (1.879)	0.065 (1.412)	yes	0.96	0.402	IRS

Plastics									
(a)	168	0.818	0.671	0.551	—	no	0.81	0.552	—
			(15.768)	(11.416)					
(b)	168	0.658	0.668	0.562	0.050	no	0.81	0.550	—
			(15.696)	(11.622)	(1.530)				
(c)	168	0.474	0.644	0.645	—	yes	0.87	0.452	—
			(12.984)	(9.818)					
(d)	168	0.427	0.634	0.644	0.048	yes	0.88	0.449	IRS
			(12.774)	(9.873)	(1.680)				
Textile spinning and weaving									
(a)	1,630	5.459	0.258	0.726	—	no	0.50	0.631	—
			(3.644)	(23.415)					
(b)	1,630	5.030	0.247	0.753	0.153	no	0.56	0.595	—
			(3.123)	(25.661)	(9.493)				
(c)	1,630	6.466	0.171	0.469	—	yes	0.62	0.548	—
			(3.851)	(12.235)					
(d)	1,630	6.059	0.162	0.256	0.157	yes	0.69	0.499	0.58
			(3.669)	(13.909)	(11.287)				
Textile products									
(a)	425	3.866	0.351	0.622	—	no	0.53	0.672	—
			(3.405)	(5.347)					
(b)	425	3.508	0.311	0.653	0.214	no	0.63	0.605	—
			(3.289)	(6.263)	(5.575)				
(c)	425	4.491	0.384	0.263	—	yes	0.75	0.495	—
			(3.879)	(2.000)					
(d)	425	5.515	0.234	0.231	0.234	yes	0.86	0.366	0.51
			(2.376)	(8.501)	(8.733)				

Table 4-1 *(continued)*

Industry		*Number of Observations* (N)	*Intercept ln A*	α	β	γ	*Inclusion of Firm Intercepts* a_i	$\bar{R}^2$	*SEE*	*Returns to Scale and Estimates of c in the case of Constant Returns to Scale (CRS)*[c]
Apparel										
	(a)	253	3.280	0.080 (2.399)	0.898 (21.834)	—	no	0.78	0.493	—
	(b)	253	2.884	0.074 (2.344)	0.915 (23.567)	0.132 (5.769)	no	0.81	0.464	—
	(c)	253	2.984	0.149 (3.212)	0.827 (12.748)	—	yes	0.80	0.468	—
	(d)	253	3.053	0.119 (2.774)	0.776 (12.925)	0.143 (6.028)	yes	0.84	0.429	0.11
Beverages										
	(a)	192	4.446	−0.063 (0.248)	1.054 (11.488)	—	no	0.61	0.869	—
	(b)	192	4.165	−0.072 (0.915)	1.065 (11.725)	0.119 (2.568)	no	0.62	0.857	—
	(c)	192	5.167	0.076 (0.869)	0.721 (6.417)	—	yes	0.82	0.588	—
	(d)	192	5.453	0.031 (0.366)	0.655 (6.104)	0.147 (4.186)	yes	0.84	0.556	n.s.

Miscellaneous publishing									
(a)	177	5.156	0.144 (2.687)	0.778 (18.209)	—	no	0.76	0.509	—
(b)	177	4.666	0.142 (2.909)	0.799 (19.821)	0.136 (14.953)	no	0.78	0.478	—
(c)	177	6.128	0.151 (3.114)	0.410 (5.043)	—	yes	0.86	0.397	—
(d)	177	5.801	0.139 (3.300)	0.414 (5.870)	0.139 (6.259)	yes	0.89	0.344	0.45

[a]regression coefficients
[b] t = values
[c]The estimates of the output elasticity with respect to management c are not provided if (1) either increasing (IRS) or decreasing (DRS) returns to scale were evidenced, or (2) if either the estimates of α or β were not statistically significant (n.s.) at the 5 percent level.

Some simple statistics tests were employed to explore the relationships between technical efficiency as measured by our efficiency index, on the one hand, and ownership, profitability, and firm size, on the other. Those tests consisted of bivariate regression analysis. Their results are reported in table 4-2. An increasing technical efficiency index for individual firms is associated with an increasing degree of technical efficiency in production relative to the industry mean. In all of the relationships explored there is no formal model which explains differing degrees of technical efficiency. Instead, our analysis merely explores some simple associations. In the statistical tests a two-tailed test of significance was employed at the 5 percent level. Since there is weak theoretical reasoning, as opposed to assertions, as to the direction of any associations between efficiency and other economic variables, a two-tailed test appears to be more appropriate than a one-tailed test.

The relationship between technical efficiency and firm ownership was analyzed with the equivalent of an analysis-of-variance test between the two variables. Ownership was defined as a dummy variable, where foreign firms = 1 and domestic firms = 0, and was used to be regressed on the technical efficiency index for each industry. As seen in table 4-2, the bivariate associations, while generally positive, were only statistically significant for two industries (textile products and beverages). It can be noted that foreign firm participation in these two industries is limited.[9] In two other industries—domestic appliances and communications equipment, and chemicals and chemical products—a positive bivariate association was significant at the 10 percent level. In view of this scanty and piecemeal evidence it seems reasonable to conclude that there is no clearcut bivariate relationship between efficiency and foreign ownership. The spotty evidence supporting a hypothesis of a positive relationship is not sufficient to justify a definitive conclusion. This is not to deny necessarily that such a relationship does not exist. It is just that our evidence, we feel, is not conclusive.[10] Moreover, the relationship as implicitly modeled here is oversimplistic.

The relationship between technical efficiency and profitability is one that is generally thought to be positive, although it might be argued that technically efficient firms are not necessarily price efficient.[11] Regressing our relative technical efficiency index on the observed firm profit rates, the regression coefficients for the included industries were generally positive but statistically insignificant. In only one industry—perfumery and cosmetics—was the relationship significant. One possible difficulty with these results may arise from the rather precarious nature of the profit data. Balance sheet information, used as our basic data source, is not subjected as a rule to vigorous independent audit, and it is widely believed in Brazil that many firms manipulate their reported profit information to their advantage. For example, it is evidently common practice for foreign firms, faced with profit repatriation fiscal restrictions, to repatriate actual profits through the overinvoicing of imports or other transfer pricing procedures.

Table 4-2
Interfirm Regressions of the Computed Technical-Efficiency Index with Other Economic Variables for Selected Manufacturing Industries, 1975 Data

Industry	*Number of Observations* (N)	*Constant*	*Foreign Firm Dummy*	*Profit Rate*	*Ln Labor*	$\bar{R}^2$
Equipment and motor machinery						
(1)	36	1.78	0.45 (1.444)[a]	—	—	0.03
(2)	36	2.07	—	−0.31 (0.190)	—	0.01
(3)	36	−0.86	—	—	0.42 (2.012)	0.08
(4)	36	−1.29	0.43 (1.428)	0.74 (0.460)	0.43 (2.010)	0.11
Electrical equipment						
(1)	22	2.40	1.78 (1.356)	—	—	0.11
(2)	22	2.70	—	2.24 (1.279)	—	0.07
(3)	22	1.16	—	—	0.031 (0.642)	0.02
(4)	22	3.33	1.53 (1.073)	2.06 (0.853)	−0.18 (0.171)	0.17
Domestic appliances and communications equipment						
(1)	26	2.57	1.24 (1.817)	—	—	0.17
(2)	26	2.91	—	0.19 (0.139)	—	0.00
(3)	26	−3.22	—	—	0.085* (3.984)	0.39
(4)	26	−1.31	0.29 (0.250)	−0.86 (0.557)	0.59 (1.105)	0.28
Chemicals and chemical products						
(1)	89	3.47	1.72 (1.949)	—	—	0.07
(2)	89	4.35	—	1.47 (0.933)	—	0.00
(3)	89	−2.19	—	—	1.03* (2.683)	0.14
(4)	89	−2.14	0.76 (0.794)	1.72 (1.140)	0.915* (2.098)	0.15
Petroleum refining						
(1)	15	179.66	187.19 (1.015)	—	—	0.00
(2)	15	542.48	—	−972.32 (1.353)	—	0.06
(3)	15	−1,220.0	—	—	237.75* (4.879)	0.62
(4)	15	−922.75	120.27 (1.025)	−707.02 (1.517)	212.23* (4.278)	0.64

Table 4-2 *(continued)*

Industry	*Number of Observations* (N)	*Constant*	*Foreign Firm Dummy*	*Profit Rate*	*Ln Labor*	$\bar{R}^2$
Pharmaceutical products						
(1)	50	0.01	0.02 (0.339)	—	—	0.00
(2)	50	0.02	—	−0.03 (0.930)	—	0.00
(3)	50	0.04	—	—	−0.46 (0.615)	0.00
(4)	50	0.05	0.02 (0.412)	−0.03 (.851)	−0.01 (0.669)	0.01
Perfumery and cosmetics						
(1)	10	2.77	−0.63 (0.643)	—	—	0.00
(2)	10	0.52	—	6.24* (3.562)	—	0.57
(3)	10	1.41	—	—	0.83* (2.337)	0.34
(4)	10	−14.212	1.29 (0.921)	−30.46 (1.303)	4.27 (1.615)	0.53
Plastics						
(1)	11	2.36	−0.87 (0.550)	—	—	0.00
(2)	11	0.97	—	4.33 (1.523)	—	0.12
(3)	11	6.88	—	—	−0.87 (1.301)	0.07
(4)	11	25.28	2.94 (0.565)	−5.21 (0.374)	−4.23 (0.867)	0.00
Textile spinning and weaving						
(1)	29	2.91	0.17 (0.251)	—	—	0.00
(2)	29	3.03	—	−0.43 (0.217)	—	0.00
(3)	29	8.04	—	—	−0.73* (5.192)	0.51
(4)	29	8.21	0.92 (2.031)	1.54 (1.167)	−0.84* (5.927)	0.56
Textile products						
(1)	13	2.67	1.70* (3.096)	—	—	0.42
(2)	13	2.56	—	1.50 (0.565)	—	0.00
(3)	13	0.72	—	—	0.31 (0.591)	0.00
(4)	13	4.98	1.93* (3.000)	1.75 (0.826)	−0.39 (0.830)	0.37

Table 4-2 *(continued)*

Industry	*Number of Observations* (N)	*Constant*	*Foreign Firm Dummy*	*Profit Rate*	*Ln Labor*	$\bar{R}^2$
Beverages						
(1)	64	1.77	0.19* (8.510)	—	—	0.53
(2)	64	0.46	—	0.55 (1.335)	—	0.01
(3)	64	−2.15	—	—	0.47* (4.111)	0.20
(4)	64	0.03	0.17* (7.854)	0.40 (1.538)	0.27* (3.190)	0.60
Miscellaneous publishing[b]						
(1)	9	3.41	—	−1.38 (0.006)	—	0.00
(2)	9	−2.05	—	—	0.77 (2.111)	0.23
(3)	9	−4.42	—	12.62 (0.363)	0.96 (1.975)	0.28

[a]The *t*-values appear in parentheses beneath the regression coefficients. The asterisks (*) indicate those coefficients which were significant at the 5 percent level in a two-tailed text.

[b]For miscellaneous publishing there were no foreign firms for which the individual firm intercept was significant.

While one would perhaps reasonably expect greater profitability for more efficient firms, our evidence, admittedly based on weak data, as noted above, suggests that there may not be a significant relationship between technical efficiency and profitability. Or it may be, as in the foreign ownership case, that there does exist a relationship, but it is more complex than apparent from our simple bivariate tests.

The relationship between a firm's relative technical efficiency and its size, as measured as the log of its labor force, is explored in equation (3) in table 4-2. As indicated, a positive relationship appears to be evident in a number of the selected industries. In five of these industries the estimated positive regression coefficients were significant. Only three industries displayed negative coefficients, and in only two of these industries—textile spinning and weaving—was the estimated regression coefficient significant. On the basis of these results we can conclude that there is some, although weak, evidence to suggest that there is a tendency for larger firms to be more efficient, as is apparent in a number of the selected industries.

Equation (4) in table 4-2 presents the results of the estimation of the regressions of the firm-specific technical efficiency index on all three independent variables for each industry. In no case is there statistical significance at the 5 percent level for all of these variables. In one industry, beverages, foreign ownership and firm size were seen to be jointly important; profitability, while also possessing a positive sign, was not quite significant.[12] In view of the results of the equation (4) estimations, with the possible exception of beverages there do not appear to be any significantly important interactions between firm ownership, profit rates, and size in determining firm relative efficiency. A caveat to this conclusion, as observed above, is that we have no specified underlying model explaining variations in efficiency. Consequently, any statistical probing, as reported here, is bound to be exploratory in nature.

Concluding Remarks

This chapter has employed the covariance model with micro data to estimate industry Cobb-Douglas production functions free of management bias for a number of Brazilian manufacturing industries. A pooled data set consisting of five annual observations for a cross-section of manufacturing firms was employed for the analysis. In all industries managerial inputs, reflecting different degrees of technical efficiency, were seen to be important, although only in those industries where the constant-returns-to-scale hypothesis could not be rejected could the output elasticity with respect to managerial inputs be computed. Estimates of the latter ranged from 0.11 to 0.58. Hicks neutral technological change was specified over the five-year period, and its annual proportional rates for different industries were estimated as being rather high, ranging from 4.8 percent to 23.6 percent annually. If such magnitudes are at all reasonable, it is apparent that technological progress during the 1971-1975 boom period was highly important in accounting for the significant growth during that period.

The individual firms intercepts, representative of firm-specific technical efficiency, were used to compute an index of technical efficiency for the firm relative to the industry mean. The analysis with the measure of efficiency took the form of simple bivariate statistical analysis between firm efficiency, on the one hand, and other firm-specific economic variables, including foreign ownership, profitability, and size, on the other. For the most part, as we have seen, these tests were inconclusive. Few clearcut and strong associations could be discerned. Only in the case of firm size was there apparent any solid suggestive evidence of a simple bivariate relationship. There is little systematic evidence from our analysis to support the frequently heard contention that foreign firms operating in Brazil, or perhaps in developing countries in general, exhibit greater levels of technical efficiency than domestically owned firms.

Finally, what should be an obvious warning is in order. One must interpret our empirical results and their subsequent analysis with extreme caution. The data base is fraught with problems. A particular concern is our inability to have incorporated intermediate inputs in the production function estimates. The analysis presented here is meant to be illustrative and exploratory rather than definitive. The analysis-of-covariance production model specified in the manner presented does, it is felt, offer some possibilities for future analysis of the technical efficiency question. It is hoped that other researchers, armed with better statistical information, will be able to go beyond our analysis and present results deserving greater confidence than ours. It is this, of course, which is the building process and function of economic research.

Notes

1. This assumption does not appear overly restrictive for a relatively short period of time. In the empirical analysis presented in this chapter the period covered is five years—not long enough for substantial structural changes to have taken place. Moreover, a firm characterized by efficient management at the beginning of the five-year period is likely to possess the same at the end of the period.

2. "Quem é Quem na Economia Brasileira," *Visão,* Edição Especial, various issues.

3. The *Visão* coverage has increased over time. Therefore, the 1975 interfirm cross-section contained more firms than the 1971 cross section.

4. The primary source for identifying foreign-owned firms was Jean Bernet, *Guia Interinvest* (Rio de Janeiro: Editôra Interinvest, 1973).

5. The possible existence of excess capacity would affect the resultant estimtes of technical efficiency. Unfortunately, no firm-specific measures of capacity utilization were available to permit the appropriate adjustments. However, with the exception of 1975 the period in question was one of vigorous industrial expansion. The year 1975, though generally considered a recession year, was characterized nevertheless by an industrial growth rate of 4 percent. Consequently, for the period 1971-1975 excess capacity is not thought to have been great. Because of demand conditions, firms had significant economic incentives to utilize productive capacity as soon as it came on line through investment.

6. It is also necessary to assume that the mean for this ratio is time-invariant. If not, the estimate λ will be biased.

7. The software system used in our calculations—SPSS—does not provide a printout of the covariance matrix, making a test of $\alpha + \beta = 1$ im-

possible with the equations reported in table 4-1. Consequently, a more direct test of $\alpha + \beta = 1$ was employed. The equation

$$\ln \left(\frac{X}{L}\right)_{ij} = \ln A + \alpha \ln \left(\frac{K}{L}\right)_{ij} + h \ln L_{ij}$$

was estimated with OLS. The parameter h equals 0 if $\alpha + \beta = 1$. Accordingly, the standard t-test for the significance of h from zero was used. A similar equation allowing for a production function shift due to Hicks neutral technological progress was also employed with similar results.

8. As in the case of the estimation of equation 4.2, alternatives with the inclusion of Hicks neutral technological progress were also estimated. This inclusion did not change the results of the tests.

9. In 1971 it was estimated that foreign firms accounted for 19 percent of total net assets in the textile products industry and 10 percent in the beverage industry (Tyler 1976, p. 52).

10. The results reported here are also consistent with those of other studies employing different estimating procedures. See Tyler (1978) and (1979).

11. For an empirical development of this argument applied to Brazil, see Samuel A. Morley and Gordon W. Smith, "Limited Search and the Technology Choices of Multinational Firms in Brazil," *Quarterly Journal of Economics*, 91, no. 2 (May 1977):263-288.

12. If a one-tailed test were applied, firm profitability would have been statistically significant at the 10 percent level in equation (4) for beverages.

Appendix A: Value of Manufacturing Output, and Tariff Protection and Export Subsidies

Table A-1
Distribution of the Value-of-Manufacturing Output, by Industry, Selected Years, 1919-1974
(percent of total)

Industry	*1919*	*1939*	*1949*	*1964*	*1968*	*1974*
Traditional Consumer Goods	78.6	68.8	66.0	46.2	40.9	34.0
Textiles	27.0	23.1	19.0	10.9	11.1	7.8
Apparel	8.2	4.7	4.4	3.0	3.0	3.3
Food	32.9	31.5	32.0	25.2	18.5	15.8
Beverages	4.7	2.6	3.1	2.1	2.0	1.3
Tobacco	3.6	1.8	1.5	1.0	1.1	0.7
Printing and Publishing	na	2.6	2.8	1.5	2.3	1.9
Furniture	1.4	1.6	1.7	1.4	1.5	1.5
Miscellaneous	0.8	0.9	1.5	1.1	1.4	1.7
Intermediate Goods	20.0	26.2	28.7	36.8	40.4	44.7
Nonmetallic minerals	2.7	3.7	4.6	4.0	4.4	3.4
Metallurgy	3.4	6.3	7.7	10.1	10.6	14.2
Lumber and wood	4.3	2.8	2.8	2.1	2.2	2.5
Paper	1.3	1.8	2.0	2.3	2.6	3.3
Rubber	0.1	0.6	1.6	2.0	2.1	1.5
Leather	2.5	1.9	1.5	0.8	0.8	0.5
Chemicals[a]	5.7	9.1	8.5	15.6	17.6	19.3
Capital Goods	1.4	5.0	5.3	17.0	18.8	21.4
Machinery	0.1	1.1	1.6	2.7	4.4	7.4
Electrical and communications equipment	.0	0.9	1.5	5.0	5.7	5.1
Transportation equipment	1.3	3.0	2.2	9.3	8.7	8.9
Total Manufacturing	100.0	100.0	100.0	100.0	100.0	100.0

Source: Industrial Censuses for 1919, 1939, and 1949. For other years data are from various IBGE industrial surveys either published in IBGE's *Produção Industrial* or *Anuário Estatístico,* various years.

[a]Chemicals in this table include the pharmaceutical products, perfumery, and plastics industries.

Table A-2
Nominal Tariff Protection and Export Subsidies, by Industry, 1977
(percent)

Industry	Nominal Tariff Protection		Nominal Export Subsidies			
	Legal Rate[a]	Realized Rate[b]	Fiscal IPI and ICM Subsidies	Income Tax Incentives	Credit Subsidies	Total
Mining	4.0	16.0	−7.7	5.4	0.0	−2.3
Extraction of combustible minerals	1.0	0.0	0.0	0.0	0.0	0.0
Cement	35.0	8.9	16.2	2.2	7.6	26.0
Glass and glass products	96.0	39.6	18.9	1.4	6.4	26.8
Other nonmetallic mineral products	75.0	47.0	15.8	0.8	6.0	22.7
Cast iron and basic steel	24.0	40.6	13.7	2.3	5.6	21.6
Rolled steel	26.0	21.3	25.0	0.9	4.0	30.0
Steel and iron foundry products	78.1	20.8	20.0	1.2	2.8	24.0
Nonferrous metals	20.0	21.4	8.3	0.5	2.4	11.3
Other metals products	53.0	37.1	22.5	1.7	4.6	29.0
Pumps and motors	52.0	26.7	25.9	0.8	3.4	30.0
Machine parts	47.0	52.3	26.8	0.9	4.8	32.4
Industrial equipment and machinery	39.0	33.0	24.1	1.5	7.7	30.4
Agricultural equipment and machinery	28.0	25.1	16.2	1.4	4.1	21.8
Office and domestic equipment and machinery	67.0	28.6	27.9	1.6	4.9	24.3
Tractors	28.0	30.1	23.4	0.2	2.6	26.7
Equipment for electric energy	73.0	44.8	20.0	0.7	8.7	29.3
Electrical conductors	67.0	36.1	20.0	1.7	7.0	28.7
Electrical equipment	62.0	54.9	20.5	1.2	4.4	26.0
Electrical machinery	27.0	26.9	25.2	0.3	3.7	29.2
Electronic equipment	47.0	25.5	20.7	0.6	3.9	25.1
Communications equipment	86.0	52.5	26.1	0.3	5.4	32.0
Automobiles	112.0	5.7	26.0	1.0	5.4	32.5
Trucks and buses	31.0	33.6	26.3	0.4	4.6	31.3
Motors and vehicle parts	91.0	22.0	25.9	1.2	3.8	30.9
Shipbuilding	9.0	21.3	24.0	1.1	8.7	32.8
Railway and aircraft equipment	42.0	24.6	24.4	2.1	5.7	32.3
Lumber and wood products	140.0	8.1	10.1	1.0	1.5	12.6
Furniture	83.0	11.4	28.0	1.0	[illegible]	[illegible]

Pump products	20.0	21.8	0.9	0.0	3.2	[illegible]
Paper and paper board	25.0	24.1	26.1	0.9	7.2	35.3
Paper products	84.0	71.9	27.6	0.3	7.0	34.9
Rubber	98.0	66.8	27.7	1.7	2.1	31.4
Leather products	155.0	28.4	9.1	0.7	1.4	11.2
Chemical products	18.0	33.9	8.0	2.6	4.8	15.3
Petroleum refining	7.0	17.9	2.1	1.4	0.0	3.9
Coal products	19.0	1.4	0.0	0.0	0.0	0.0
Resins and synthetic fibers	42.0	19.8	25.2	4.7	4.6	30.1
Vegetable oils	64.0	8.0	8.0	3.9	3.9	4.0
Paints and varnishes	54.0	19.1	15.3	4.4	4.4	20.6
Miscellaneous chemical products	20.0	4.6	17.0	3.6	3.6	21.9
Pharmaceutical products	18.0	17.2	7.5	6.2	6.2	14.5
Perfumery and soaps	55.0	20.9	21.5	4.4	4.4	26.0
Plastics	122.0	60.7	25.2	3.7	3.7	29.9
Natural fiber preparations	53.0	9.0	8.2	1.5	1.6	11.2
Synthetic fiber testile mill products	63.0	15.6	35.5	4.1	4.1	41.0
Natural fiber textile mill products	184.0	35.6	31.6	6.4	6.4	39.3
Other textile products, including knitting	64.0	26.5	31.5	9.4	9.4	42.1
Apparel	176.00	12.6	27.8	8.3	8.3	37.5
Footwear	170.0	37.3	12.0	9.4	9.4	23.0
Food products	55.0	1.5	6.1	3.1	3.1	10.1
Sugar refining	84.0	0.0	5.0	0.0	0.0	5.7
Refined vegetable oil products	65.0	22.3	6.3	13.7	13.7	20.1
Other food products	115.0	15.1	21.2	2.7	2.7	25.2
Beverages	187.0	80.0	25.1	5.6	3.7	31.4
Tobacco	154.0	63.6	−5.3	4.1	0.0	−1.2
Printing and publishing	5.0	5.1	20.2	5.5	0.4	26.1
Miscellaneous manufacturing	42.0	15.1	22.1	1.3	1.3	28.9
Manufacturing average[c]	67.9	33.3	18.6	1.1	5.0	24.8

Source: FUNCEX Materials. José Augusto Arantes Savasini et al., "Acompanhamento da quantificação da Estrutura de Incentivos às Exportações: Efeitos da Política Protecionista Após 1975, Fundação Centro de Estudos do Comércio Exterior, unpublished paper, 1979, p. 9 and Joal de Azambuja Rosa et al., "Alguns Aspectos da Política Tarifária Recente", Fundação Centro de Estudos do Comércio Exterior, unpublished paper, November 1979, p. 92.

[a]Import weighted averages.

[b]The realized tariff rate is equal to the tariff collections divided by the CIF value of imports. In their case it also includes the realized import deposit tariff equivalents.

[c]Value added weights from the 1970 input-output table were used.

Appendix B: Capital-Goods Industries

Table B-1
Tariff Protection for the Brazilian Capital-Goods Industries, 1974
(percent)

Industry	*Nominal Tariff Rate*[a]	*Realized Tariff Rate*[b]
Large, custom-made machinery and equipment	42.7	5.3
Standardized machinery and equipment	36.0	5.1
Machine tools	32.0	4.5
Textile machinery	38.5	5.4
Office machinery	23.0	3.2
Other machinery	40.5	5.7
Machine parts and accessories	47.6	5.7
Large, custom-made electrical machinery and equipment	51.1	6.3
Standardized electrical machinery and equipment	75.6	10.6
Generators, motors, transformers, and other equipment	58.4	7.2
Electrical control equipment	48.5	6.0
Telecommunications equpment	105.3	14.2
Parts and accessories for electrical machinery and equipment	48.1	6.1
Tools for cutting and farming	42.5	9.5
Instruments	28.7	9.6
Optical instruments	31.4	10.4
Scientific instruments	18.2	6.2
Trucks and buses	63.0	7.1
Tractors	32.8	4.0
Railway equipment	26.0	0.2
Shipbuilding	8.8	0.5
Aircraft	35.6	0.7
Vehicle parts and accessories	58.3	8.1
Capital-Goods Industries Average	40.8	6.1

Source: Marcos G. Fonseca, Akihiro Ikeda, and José Paulo Z. Chahad, *Pesquisa Complementar sobre Substituição de Importação de Bens de Capital,* FIPE, Parte A, Fevereiro 1978, pp. 203-204.

Table B-2
CACEX Participation Agreements, by Sector, 1977

Sectors	Number of Agreements and Revisions	Total Capital Goods Amount Negotiated (U.S. $ million)	Percentage Share of Capital Goods	
			To be Purchased Domestically	To be Imported
Mining	5	121.4	74.5	25.5
Nonmetallic minerals	7	49.3	84.0	16.0
Metallurgy	49	903.8	74.9	25.1
Machinery	31	187.3	61.6	38.4
Electrical machinery	5	7.6	95.9	4.1
Transportation equipment	19	144.7	70.3	29.7
Paper	12	209.8	80.2	19.8
Leather	1	0.3	73.3	26.7
Chemicals	53	363.1	78.4	21.6
Food products	3	30.4	87.2	12.8
Miscellaneous manufactures	1	1.4	69.3	30.7
Electric energy	3	67.9	76.3	23.7
Transportation	2	798.6	81.2	18.8
Communications	1	53.9	69.6	30.4
Total	192	2,938.5	76.6	23.4

Source: CACEX.

Table B-3
Nominal Subsidies to Capital-Goods Exports, 1975
(percent)

IBGE Sector Classification Code	*Industry*	*(1) Fiscal Subsidies as percent of exported Unit Value*	*(2) Credit Subsidies as percent of Exported Unit Value*	*(3) Total Export Subsidies as percent of Exported Unit Value*
121	Pumps and motors	22.4	0.1	22.5
122	Machine parts	20.8	—	20.8
123	Industrial equipment and machinery	21.0	13.5	34.5
124	Agricultural equipment and machinery	16.8	10.9	27.8
125	Office and domestic equipment and machinery	24.9	2.0	26.9
126	Tractors	23.0	13.5	36.5
131	Equipment for electric energy	19.4	2.1	21.5
132	Electric conductors	20.0	1.4	21.4
133	Electrical equipment	20.2	4.5	24.7
134	Electrical machinery	25.7	4.6	30.3
135	Electronic equipment	20.0	—	20.0
136	Communications equipment	26.5	5.0	31.5
142	Trucks and buses	26.0	9.7	35.7
143	Motors and vehicle parts	25.8	4.3	30.1
144	Shipbuilding	23.5	5.9	29.4
145	Railway and aircraft equipment	15.5	7.3	22.3

Source: Affonso Celso Pastore, José Augusto Arantes Savasini and Joal de Azambuja Rosa, "Quantificação dos Incentivos às Exportacões," Fundação Centro de Estudos do Comércio Exterior, Rio de Janeiro, 1977, p. 33.

Appendix C: Manufacturing Establishments

Table C-1
Participation of Small, Medium, and Large Manufacturing Establishments according to Value of Output, 1970

	Number of Establishments (N)		*Value of Production (X)*		*Employment[b] (L)*		*Salaries (W)*		*Taxes,*	*Value Added*	
Size Class[a]	*N*	*Percent of Total*	*Cr$ Million*	*Percent of Total*	*Number*	*Percent of Total*	*Cr$ Million*	*Percent of Total*	*Percent of Total*	*Cr$ Million*	*Percent of Total*
Small (Total)	135,008	95.0	19,012	21.2	915,278	44.1	2,647	28.5	15.0	9,063	22.4
1- 640	98,361	69.3	2,915	3.3	321,331	15.5	450	4.9	1.7	1,439	3.6
641- 1,000	10,279	7.2	1,545	1.7	75,498	3.6	220	2.4	1.0	720	1.8
1,001- 3,000	17,649	12.4	5,675	6.3	231,655	11.2	814	8.8	4.5	2,717	6.7
3,001-10,000	8,719	6.1	8,877	9.9	286,794	13.8	1,163	12.5	7.8	4,187	10.4
Medium 10,000-70,000	5,362	3.8	24,634	27.5	604,652	19.1	2,794	30.1	23.9	11,183	27.7
Large Above 70,000	1,043	.7	45,976	51.3	553,741	26.7	3,835	41.3	61.1	20,171	49.8
Total[d]	142,110	100.0	89,622	100.0	2,074,911	100.0	9,276	100.0	100.0	40,417	100.0

Source: Special IBGE tabulations from the 1970 economic census made for CEBRAE.

[a]According to the value of the establishment's production (measured in multiples of the minimum wage).

[b]Includes all economically active personnel.

[c]Includes the payment of IPI and ICM taxes, as recorded in the census.

[d]The totals may differ slightly from the sums of the listed components due to rounding and some data omission.

Table C-2
Regional Distribution of Brazilian Manufacturing Establishments, Employment, and Output, 1970
(percent share of total)

Region	*Number of Establishments*	*Total Employees*	*Total Salaries and Wages*	*Value of Output*	*Value Added*
North	1.9	1.5	0.8	0.9	1.0
Northeast	18.8	10.2	5.6	6.4	5.8
Center-south	51.8	69.7	80.3	78.3	79.5
South	23.0	16.9	11.8	12.8	11.9
Center-west	4.4	1.4	0.7	1.1	0.8
Total	100.0	100.0	100.0	100.0	100.0

Source: IBGE, *Censo Industrial: Brasil, 1970.*

Note: Because of rounding totals may not add up to 100 percent.

Bibliography

Aigner, Dennis J.; Knox Lovell, C.A. and Schmidt, Peter. "Formulation and Estimation of Stochastic Frontier Production Function Models." *Journal of Econometrics* 6 (1977):21-37.

Almeida, José. *A Implantação da Indústria Automobilístic no Brasil.* Rio de Janeiro: Fundação Getúlio Vargas, 1972.

de Azambuja Rosa, Joal, et al. "Alguns Aspectos da Política Tarifária Recente." Fundação Centro de Estudos do Comércio Exterior. Unpublished paper, November 1979.

Bacha, Edmar Lisboa; da Mata, Milton; and Modenesi, Rui Lyrio. *Encargos Trabalhistas e Absorção de Mão-de-Obra: Uma Interpretação do Problema e seu Debate.* Relatório de Pesquisa no. 12. Rio de Janeiro: IPEA/INPES, 1972.

Baer, Werner. *The Development of the Brazilian Steel Industry.* Nashville, Tennessee: Vanderbilt University Press, 1969.

______. "Import Substitution and Industrialization in Latin America: Experiences and Interpretations." *Latin American Research Review* 7, no. 1 (Spring, 1972):95-122.

______. *Industrialization and Economic Development in Brazil.* Homewood, Illinois: Richard D. Irwin, 1965.

Baer, Werner, and Hervé, Michel. "Employment and Industrialization in Developing Countries." *Quarterly Journal of Economics* 70, no. 1 (February 1966):88-107.

Baer, Werner; Kerstenetsky, Isaac; and Villela, Annibal V. "The Changing Role of the State in the Brazilian Economy." *World Development* 1, no. 11 (November, 1973).

Baer, Werner, and Geiger, Pedro Pincas. "Industrialização, Urbanização e a Persistência das Desigualdades Regionais no Brasil" in Werner Baer, Pedro Pincas Geiger and Paulo Roberto Haddad, eds. *Dimensões do Desenvolvimento Brasileiro.* Rio de Janeiro: Editôra Campus, 1978: 65-150.

Baer, Werner; Newfarmer, Richard; and Trebat, Thomas J. "Considerações sobre o Capitalismo Estatal no Brasil: Algumas Questões e Problemas Novos." *Pesquisa e Planejamento Econômico* 6, no. 3 (December 1976):727-752.

Balassa, Bela, et al. *The Structure of Protection in Developing Countries.* Baltimore: Johns Hopkins University Press, 1971.

Bergsman, Joel. "Foreign Trade Policy and Development." In H. Jon Rosenbaum and William G. Tyler, eds. *Contemporary Brazil: Issues in Economic and Political Development.* New York: Frederick A. Praeger, 1972.

Bergsman, Joel. *Brazil: Industrialization and Trade Policies.* London: Oxford University Press, 1970.

______. "Commercial Policy, Allocation Efficiency, and 'X-Efficiency'." *Quarterly Journal of Economics.* 78, no. 3 (August, 1974):410-433.

Bergsman, Joel, and Malan, Pedro. "A Estrutura de Proteção Industrial no Brasil." *Revista Brasileira de Economia.* 24, no. 2 (Junho 1970). Reprinted in English in Bela Balassa and Associates. *The Structure of Protection in Developing Countries.* Baltimore: The Johns Hopkins Press, 1971.

Bernet, Jean. *Guia Interinvest.* Rio de Janeiro: Editora Interinvest, 1973.

Bonelli, Regis. "Technology and Growth in Brazilian Manufacturing." *Brazilian Economic Studies* no. 2 (1976):35-72.

______. *Tecnologia e Crescimento Industrial: A Experiência Brasileira nos Anos 60.* Monografia no. 25. Rio de Janeiro: IPEA/INPES, 1976.

Bonelli, Regis, and Façanha, Luiz Otávio. "A Indústria de Bens de Capital no Brasil: Desenvolvimento, Problemas e Perspectivas." In Wilson Suzigan, ed. *Indústria: Política, Instituições e Desenvolvimento.* Monografia no. 28. Rio de Janeiro: IPEA/INPES, 1978.

Bonelli, Regis, and Werneck, Dorothea. "Desempenho Industrial: Auge e Desaceleração nos Anos 70." In Wilson Suzigan, ed. *Indústria: Política, Instituições e Desenvolvimento.* Monograph no. 28. Rio de Janeiro: IPEA/INPES, 1979:167-226.

Candal, Arthur, et al. *A Industrialização Brasileira: Diagnóstico e Perspectivas.* Programa Estratégico de Desenvolvimento, 1968-1970. Rio de Janeiro: Ministério do Planejamento e Coordenação Geral, 1969.

Carneiro Netto, Dionísio Dias. "Política de Controle de Preços Industriais: Perspectiva Teórica e Análise Institucional Brasileira." In Fernando Resende and Jorge Vianna Monteiro, eds. *Aspectos da Participação do Governo na Economia.* Monografia no. 26. Rio de Janeiro: IPEA/INPES, 1976:135-173.

de Castelo Branco, Flávio Pinheiro. *Importações de Bens de Capital e Substituição de Importações.* Master's thesis, University of Brasília, 1976.

Cavalcanti de Albuquerque, Roberto, and Cavalcanti, Clóvis de Vasconcelos. *Desenvolvimento Regional no Brasil.* Estudos para o Planejamento no. 16. Brasília: IPEA/INPES, 1976.

Clark, Paul. "Brazilian Import Liberalization." Mimeographed paper prepared for AID, September 1967.

Cline, William R. *Potential Effects of Income Redistribution on Economic Growth: Latin American Cases.* New York: Frederick A. Praeger, 1972.

von Doellinger, Carlos, et al. "Considerações à Política Cambial Brasileira Pós-1973." IPLAN/IPEA, unpublished paper, November 1979.

von Doellinger, Carlos, and Cavalcanti, Leonardo C. *Empresas Multinacionais na Indústria Brasileira*. Relatório de Pesquisa no. 29. Rio de Janeiro: IPEA/INPES, 1975.

von Doellinger, Carlos; de Castro Faria, Hugo B.; Ramos, Raimundo Nonato Mendonça; and Cavalcanti, Leonardo Caserta. *Transformações da Estrutura das Exportações Brasileiras: 1964/70*. Relatório de Pesquisa no. 14. Rio de Janeiro: IPEA/INPES, 1973.

von Doellinger, Carlos; de Castro Faria, Hugo B.; and Cavalcanti, Leonardo Caserta. *A Política Brasileira de Comércio Exterior e seus Efeitos: 1967/73*. Relatório de Pesquisa no. 22. Rio de Janeiro: IPEA/INPES, 1974.

Donnelly, John T. "External Financing and Short-Term Consequences of External Debt Servicing for Brazilian Economic Development, 1947-1968." *The Journal of Developing Areas* 7, no. 3 (April 1973).

Eckaus, Richard S. "The Factor Proportions Problem in Underdeveloped Areas." *American Economic Review*. 45, no. 4 (September 1955):195-214.

Evans, Peter. *Dependent Development: The Alliance of Multinational, State, and Local Capital in Brazil*. Princeton, New Jersey: Princeton University Press, 1979.

Farrell, M.J. "The Measurement of Productive Efficiency." *Journal of the Royal Statistical Society*, Series A. 120, Part 3 (1957):253-290.

Fendt, Roberto. *The Experience of Developing Countries as Importers of Manufactures from Developing Countries: Brazil*. Significant Issues Series. Washington: Center for Strategic and International Studies at Georgetown University, 1981.

Fishlow, Albert. "Brazilian Size Distribution of Income." *American Economic Review*. Papers and Proceedings 62, no. 2 (May 1971):391-402.

______. "Origins and Consequences of Import Substitution in Brazil." In Luiz Eugenio di Marco, ed., *International Economics and Development: Essays in Honor of Raul Prebisch*. New York: Academic Press, 1972.

Fonesca, Marcos G.; Ikeda, Akihiro; and Chahad, José Paulo Z. *Pesquisa Complementar sobre Substituição de Importação de Bens de Capital*. FIPE, part A, Fevereiro 1978.

Furtado, Celso. *Um Projeto para o Brasil*. Rio de Janeiro: Editôra Saga, 1968.

Gerschenkron, Alexander. *Economic Backwardness in Historical Perspective*. Cambridge, Massachusetts: Harvard University Press, 1962.

Goodman, David E., and Cavalcanti de Albuquerque, Roberto. *A Industrialização do Nordeste*. Relatório de Pesquisa 1, no. 6. Rio de Janeiro: IPEA/INPES, 1971.

Goodman, David E., and Cavalcanti de Albuquerque, Roberto *Incentivos á Industrialização e Desenvolvimento do Nordeste*. Relatório de Pesquisa no. 20. Rio de Janeiro: IPEA/INPES, 1974.

Goodman, David E.; Sena, Julio F.; and Cavalcanti de Albuquerque, Roberto. "Os Incentivos Financeiros à Industrialização no Nordeste." *Pesquisa e Planejamento* 1, no. 2 (December 1971):329-365.

Griliches, Zvi, and Ringstad, V. *Economies of Scale and the Form of the Production Function.* Amsterdam: North-Holland Publishing Company, 1971.

Gunter, Dan L., and Emerson, Robert D. "A Production Function for Florida Foliage Nurseries from Time-Series and Cross-Section Data." *Southern Journal of Agricultural Economics.* 9 (July 1977):151-156.

Hoch, Irving. "Estimation of Production Function Parameters and Testing for Efficiency." *Econometrica.* 23 (July 1955):325-326.

Hoffman, Rudolfo, and Duarte, João Carlos. "A Distribuição da Renda no Brasil." *Revista de Administração de Empresas.* 12, no. 2 (June 1972):46-66.

Jaspersen, Frederick Z. "Foreign Investment in Brazil." Mimeographed paper written for AID, Rio de Janeiro, 1970.

Knight, Peter T., et al. *Brazil: Human Resources Special Report.* Latin America and the Caribbean Regional Office, The World Bank. Washington: The World Bank, October 1979.

Langoni, Carlos Geraldo. "Distribuição da Renda e Desenvolvimento Economico do Brasil." *Estudos Econômicos.* 2, no. 5 (December 1972):5-88.

______. "A Fontes do Crescimento Econômico Brasileiro." *Estudos Econômicos.* 2, no. 4 (August 1972):3-34.

______. "A Rentabilidade dos Investimentos em Capital Físico no Brasil." *Estudos Econômicos.* 1, no. 3 (1971).

Lee, Lung-Fei, and Tyler, William G. "The Stochastic Frontier Production Function and Average Efficiency: An Empirical Analysis." *Journal of Econometrics.* 7, no. 2 (May 1978):385-389.

Leff, Nathaniel H. *The Brazilian Capital Goods Industry 1929-1964.* Cambridge, Massachusetts: Harvard University Press, 1968.

Lessa, Carlos. "Fifteen Years of Economic Policy in Brazil." *Economic Bulletin for Latin America.* 4, no. 2 (November 1964).

Lodder, Celsius A. "Estrutura Espacial, Política de Industrialização e o Problema Regional." In Wilson Suzigan, ed. *Indústria: Política, Instituições e Desenvolvimento.* Monografia no. 28. Rio de Janeiro: IPEA/INPES, 1978.

Lopes, Francisco Lafaiete. "Desigualdade e Crescimento: Um Modelo de Programação com Aplicação ao Brasil." *Pesquisa e Planejamento Econômico.* 2, no. 2 (December 1972):189-226.

Mahar, Dennis J. *Frontier Development Policy in Brazil: A Study of Amazonia.* New York: Praeger Publishers, 1979.

Maneschi, Andrea, and Nunes, Egas Moniz. "Função de Produção Agregada e Progresso Tecnológico na Economia Brasileira." *Revista de Teoria e Pesquisa Econômica.* 1, no. 1 (April 1970):77-91.

Masson, Francis. "Protection, Prices and Efficiency in the Brazilian Electrical Appliance Industry." Mimeographed paper written for AID, Rio de Janeiro, July 1970.

da Mata, Milton. "Controles de Preços na Economia Brasileira: Aspectos Institucionais e Resultados." *Pesquisa e Planejamento Econômico.* 10, no. 3 (December 1980).

______. "Crescimento Industrial e Absorção de Mão-de-Obra." In Wilson Suzigan, ed. *Indústria: Política, Instituições e Desenvolvimento.* Monografia no. 28. Rio de Janeiro: IPEA/INPES, 1978:283-308.

Meeusen, W., and van den Broeck, J. "Efficiency Estimation for Cobb-Douglas Production Functions with Composed Error." *International Economic Review.* 18, no. 2 (June 1977):515-521.

Meller, Patrícia. "Efficiency Frontiers for Industrial Establishments of Different Sizes." *Explorations in Economic Research.* 3, no. 3 (Summer 1976):379-407.

Mendonça de Barros, José Roberto; Lobato, Helenamaria; Trávolo, Maria Angélica; and Zockun, Maria Helena Garcia Pallares. "Sistema Fiscal e Incentivos às Exportações." Mimeographed paper prepared for IPE, November 1973.

Monnerat, Suely Barbosa. "Comércio Externo na Área de Bens de Capital — Período: 1973-76." EMBRAMEC. November 1977. Unpublished report.

Morley, Samuel A., and Smith, Gordon W. "Import Substitution and Foreign Investment in Brazil." *Oxford Economic Papers.* 23, no. 1 (March 1971):120-135.

Morley, Samuel A., and Smith, Gordon W. "Limited Search and Technology Choices of Multinational Firms in Brazil." *Quarterly Journal of Economics.* 91, no. 2 (May 1977):263-288.

______. "On the Measurement of Import Substitution." *American Economic Review.* 60, no. 4 (September 1970):728-735.

______. "The Effect of Changes in the Distribution of Income on Labor, Foreign Investment, and Growth in Brazil." In Alfred Stepan, ed. *Authoritarian Brazil: Origins, Policies, and Future.* New Haven: Yale University Press, 1973:119-141.

Morley, Samuel A., and Williamson, Jeffrey G. "Demand, Distribution, and Employment: The Case of Brazil." *Economic Development and Cultural Change.* 23, no. 1 (October 1974):33-60.

Mundlak, Yair. "Empirical Production Function Free of Management Bias." *Journal of Farm Economics.* 43, no. 1 (February 1961):44-56.

Neuhaus, Paulo, and Lobato, Helenamaria. "Proteção Efetiva à Indústria no Brasil, 1973-1975." Fundação Centro de Estudos do Comércio Exterior. Rio de Janeiro, unpublished manuscript, 1978.

O'Brien, F.S., and Salm, C.L. "Desemprêgo e Subemprêgo no Brasil." *Revista Brasileira de Economia.* 24, no. 4 (December 1970).

Pastore, Affonso Celso, et al. "Análise da Promoção de Exportações sob a Ótica da Proteção Efetiva." Fundação Centro de Estudos do Comércio Exterior, Rio de Janeiro, unpublished manuscript, 1977.

Pastore, Affonso Celso; Savasini, José Augusto Arantes; and de Azambuja Rosa, Joal. "Quantificação dos Incentivos às Exportações." Fundação Centro de Estudos do Comércio Exterior, Rio de Janeiro, unpublished manuscript, 1977.

Pastore, Affonso Celso; de Barros, José Roberto M.; and Kadota, Décio. "Sobre a Taxa de Câmbio: Resultados Adicionais e uma Réplica à Análise de Bacha." *Pesquisa e Planejamento Econômico.* 8, no. 2 (August 1978):457-474.

Pignaton, Alvaro A.G. "Capital Estrangeiro e Expansão Industrial no Brasil." Departamento de Economia, Universidade de Brasília, Textos para Discussão. no. 10, September 1973.

Rattner, Henrique, et al. *Pequena e Média Empresa no Brasil: 1963-1976.* Sao Paulo, unpublished book manuscript, May 1978.

Rebouças, Osmundo Evangelista, et al. "Desenvolvimento do Nordeste: Diagnóstico e Sugestões de Políticas." *Revista Econômica do Nordeste.* 10, no. 2 (June 1979):189-430.

Rezende da Silva, Fernando A., and Silva, Maria da Conceição. *O Sistema Tributário e as Desigualdades Regionais: Uma Análise da Recente Controvérsia sobre o ICM.* Monograph no. 13. Rio de Janeiro: IPEA/INPES, 1974.

Richmond, J. "Estimating the Efficiency of Production." *International Economic Review.* 15, no. 2 (June 1974):515-521.

Riedel, James, and Tyler, William G. "Export Oriented Industrialization and National Economic Integration in Brazil and Taiwan." *Viertel Jahres Berichte.* no. 75 (March 1979):35-60.

Robalinho de Barros, Frederico. "O Problema do Financiamento à Pequena e Média Indústria no País." Unpublished IPEA/INPES report, December 1974.

Robalinho de Barros, Frederico, and Modenesi, Rui Lyrio. *Pequenas e Médias Indústrias: Análise dos Problemas Incentivos e sua Contribuição ao Desenvolvimento.* Relatório de Pesquisa no. 17. Rio de Janeiro: IPEA/INPES, 1973.

Rosenbaum, H. Jon, and Tyler, William G., eds. *Contemporary Brazil: Issues in Economic and Political Development.* New York: Praeger Publishers, 1972.

Savasini, José Augusto A. *Export Promotion: The Case of Brazil*. New York: Praeger Publishers, 1978.

Savasini, José Augusto Arantes, et al. "Acompanhamento da Quantificação da Estrutura de Incentivos às Exportações: Efeitos da Política Protecionista após 1975." Fundação Centro de Estudos do Comércio Exterior. Unpublished paper, 1979.

Savasini, José Augusto A., and Kume, Honório. "Análise da Política de Promoção de Exportação segundo o Custo dos Recursos Domésticos por Unidade de Divisa Gerada." Fundação Centro de Estudos do Comércio Exterior. Rio de Janeiro, unpublished paper, 1978.

Staley, Eugene, and Morse, Richard. *Modern Small Industry for Developing Countries*. New York: McGraw Hill, 1965.

Suzigan, Wilson, "As Empresas do Governo e o Papel do Estado na Economia Brasileira." In Fernando Resende and Jorge Viana Monteiro, eds. *Aspectos da Participação do Governo na Economia*. Monograph no. 26. Rio de Janeiro: IPEA/INPES, 1976:77-134.

______. "Política Industrial no Brasil." In Wilson Suzigan, ed. *Indústria: Política, Instituições e Desenvolvimento*. Monograph no. 28. Rio de Janeiro: IPEA/INPES, 1978.

______. "Políticas de Promoção Industrial: Os Incentivos Fiscais e Financeiros." IPEA/INPES, Textos para Discussão Interna no. 26. October 1980.

Suzigan, Wilson; Bonelli, Regis; Horta, Maria Helena T.T.; and Lodder, Celsius Antonio. *Crescimento Industrial no Brasil: Incentivos e Desempenho Recente*. Relatório de Pesquisa no. 26. Rio de Janeiro: IPEA/INPES, 1974.

Suzigan, Wilson; Pereira, José Eduardo de Carvalho; and de Almeida, Ruy Affonso Guimarães. *Financiamento de Projetos Industriais no Brasil*. Relatório de Pesquisa no. 9. Rio de Janeiro: IPEA/INPES, 1972.

Tavares, Maria da Conceição. "The Growth and Decline of Import Substitution in Brazil." *Economic Bulletin for Latin America*. 4, no. 1 (March 1964).

Tendler, Judith. *Electric Power in Brazil: Entrepreneurship in the Public Sector*. Cambridge, Massachusetts: Harvard University Press, 1968.

Thoumi, Francisco E. "A Report on the Size Structure of Industry in Brazil with Special Reference to Small-Scale Industry." World Bank. Unpublished paper, November 3, 1973.

Timmer, C. Peter. "Using a Probabilistic Frontier Production Function to Measure Technical Efficiency." *Journal of Political Economy*. 79, no. 4 (July/August 1971):776-794.

Tolosa, Hamilton C. "Diferenciais de Produtividade Industrial e Estrutura Urbana." *Pesquisa e Planejamento Econômico*. 4, no. 2 (June 1974):325-352.

Tyler, William G. *Advanced Developing Countries as Export Competitors in Third World Markets: The Brazilian Experience*. Significant Issues Series. Washington: Center for Strategic and International Studies at Georgetown University, 1980.

______. "Dependent Growth and Multinational Firms in Brazil." *Ibero-Americano*. 7, no. 1 (1977):21-36.

______. "Labor Absorption with Import Substituting Industrialization: An Examination of Elasticities of Substitution in the Brazilian Manufacturing Sector." *Oxford Economic Papers*. 26, no. 1 (March 1974):93-103.

______. *Manufactured Export Expansion and Industrialization in Brazil*. Tubingen: J.C.B. Mohr, 1976.

______. "A Substituição de Importações e a Expansão de Exportações como as 'Fontes' de Crescimento Industrial no Brasil." *Revista de Estudos Econômicos*. 3, no. 5 (December 1973).

______. "Recent Effective Tariff Protection for Brazil." *Revista de Estudos Econômicos*. 10, no. 3 (December 1980a):47-59.

______. "Technical Efficiency in Production in a Developing Country: An Empirical Examination of the Brazilian Plastics and Steel Industries." *Oxford Economic Papers*. 31, no. 3 (November 1979):477-495.

______. "The Anti-Export Bias in Commercial Policies and Export Performance: Some Evidence from the Recent Brazilian Experience." IPEA/INPES, *Textos para Discussão Interna*. no. 17, May 1980b.

Vidossich, Franco. *A Indústria de Máquinas-Ferramenta no Brasil*. Rio de Janeiro: IPEA/INPES, 1974.

Villela, Annibal. "As Empresas do Govêrno Federal e sua Importância na Economia Nacional." *Revista Brasileira de Economia*. 16, no. 1 (March 1962).

Villela, Annibal, and Baer, Werner. *O Setor Privado Nacional: Problemas e Políticas para seu Fortalecimento*. Relatório de Pesquisa no. 46. Rio de Janeiro: IPEA/INPES, 1980.

Index

About the Author

William G. Tyler is a member of the faculty in the economics department at the University of Florida, where he has been affiliated since 1969. He is currently engaged as a senior economist in the Research Institute (IPEA/INPES) of the Brazilian Planning Secretariat in Rio de Janeiro. He did his undergraduate work in economics at Dickinson College and his graduate study at the Fletcher School of Law and Diplomacy, where he received the Ph.D. in 1969. From 1966 to 1969 he was a visiting professor of economics at the Brazilian School of Public Administration at the Getulio Vargas Foundation, and from 1972 to 1974 he was a senior Fellow at the Kiel Institute of World Economics at Kiel University. In 1977 Dr. Tyler was a visiting professor at Uppsala University in Sweden. He has done consulting work with the World Bank, the Brazilian Institute of Economics, AID, and private industry. His most recent books are *Manufactured Export Expansion and Industrialization in Brazil* (1976) and *Issues and Prospects for the New International Economic Order* (1977). In addition, Dr. Tyler's numerous contributions to professional journals have covered a wide range of topics in economic development and international economics, appearing in such journals as *Economic Development and Cultural Change, Oxford Economic Papers, Review of Economics and Statistics, International Organization, Journal of Econometrics, Journal of Development Studies,* and *World Development*.